Difference

Rosemary Argente

First edition 2017

Editor: Venus Alae-Carew

Cover: By Brian Sherman

ISBN: 978-09557327-4-4

Publishers: Asaina Books
Website: asainabooks.co.uk
Email: rosa@asainabooks.co.uk

Books by the same author:

Blantyre and Yawo Women
The Veil
The Promised Land – Companion to The
Veil
Praying Mantis
Broken Temple
Praying Mantis
Difference
Share the Ride
Home From Home
Essays and Poetry
The Place Beyond
Caesar and Mapanga Homestead

Novels:
All Mine to Have
Farewell Sophomore
The Stream of Memory
A British Throne Scandal

Science Fiction:
Farewell to the Aeroplane

Booklets:
Journey of Discovery
Enduring Fountain – Health and Well-being
Katherine of the Wheel
Cooking With Asaina

"The simple conception of an object, and the belief of it, and as this difference lies not in the parts or composition of the idea which we conceive it, it follows, that it must lie in the manner in which we conceive it."

David Hume – *Treatise of Human Nature.*

CONTENTS

ACKNOWLEDGEMENTS

My sincere thanks are due to Venus Alae-Carew for editing the manuscript and for our general discussions; to Ian Upton, David Duddle, Brian Sherman, and Mark Sherman for their invaluable help on my struggles with technology; also to persons too numerous to mention, transcending the cultures, for giving me much of their time in our discussions to share their personal views on the differences that exist in our world.

SOURCES:

Much of the information for this work is from eighty plus years of participant observation; various oral testimony; literature; and media reports on current and contemporaneous incidents.

PROLOGUE

The observation of human behaviour can be applied to all societies in any given situation wherever there are people. Up to the late twentieth century a chosen society could be studied in isolation from other world societies. Like most things, societies evolve over centuries, though there is still a small number that has remained untouched by evolution. In this context the term `evolution' is applied to describe changes that take place with the passage of time and not as seen by evolutionists: what may have been unacceptable in one era becomes acceptable in another or vice versa.

The estimated total number of people may depend on the length of time humans are thought to have been on Earth. From the era of agriculture, about 8000 BC, the world population may have been around 5 million, possibly 300 million in 1 CE. According to the United Nations, there were seven billion in 2011; and the US Census Bureau made a lower estimate of seven billion in March 2012. And, there are approximately 2,000 births a day. This must have its consequent effect on the evolution of societies. It is almost impossible for any society to escape evolution, at least in part, due to migration, intermarriage or other factors and the phasing out of current ideals as people pass away.

Every aspect of human existence, including the environment; increased inter-mingling of people; globalisation in human relations; and easy access to global travel, has had their impact upon world cultures, and how humans regard one another.

For one who has travelled much, enjoyed hospitality transcending cultures, and with a passionate interest in people and their origins, I have found that *difference* in people has and still plays a vital role. Though the characteristic of *difference* itself has also evolved with the passage of time.

Any social standard carries a *difference*, leading to assumed human stereotypes, and in turn fuels distinctions. Moral assessments of individuals or groups of people, lead to *inclusion* or *exclusion* within an established *status quo.* Exclusion is usually on a ground of some *difference,* and is a kind of *benign apartheid.*

In describing past events, it has been impossible to avoid certain labels once popularly accepted and designated as the accepted norm in reference to people which now seem pejorative. I have recounted my observations without fear or favour and above all without prejudice.

****

1 - UNITED KINGDOM

United Kingdom (UK) is a phrase of political expediency, a misnomer socially, there is a social and economic division south and north of the United Kingdom.

The United Kingdom is united by the language which divides it, *difference* in accents, disunited by the class system and divisions within. If the northerners move to the south in whatever they choose to engage in, they must lose their northern accent or forfeit success at their own peril.

This accent aspect applies to the whole of Britain and other countries that were exposed to Britishness and the English language.

It is also equally impossible to define Britishness without mention of the infiltration of other Caucasian races from other parts of Europe, and in more recent years, infiltration of persons from former empires and their impact on Britishness.

As David Starkey says:

> *"...it is impossible to teach Britishness because a British nation does not exist"*.

Mark Easton says:

> *"...to define Britishness is like painting the wind."*

Perhaps there is no other word or phrase in the English language that is so topical and misunderstood as `Britishness' coupled with the phrase 'social cohesion' whatever that means. This may be due to lack of understanding of the historical development and the characteristic of British society and the effect of Roman legacy upon it.

English is exclusionary to Welsh, Scottish and Irish. As Norman Davis (*The Isles*) puts it,

> "British familiarity with horse-breeding influenced the thought of human breeds in the confusion of race with nation."

Trumpeted by the Labour Party in 1999 the Scottish Parliament and Welsh Assembly entrenched their national identity and the boundaries between English, Scottish and Welsh gained momentum, rather than the opposite, as a people belonging to one nationality. The British inclusion and exclusion characteristic of administration was extended beyond the United Kingdom. It is not easy to analyse Britishness or Englishness without looking at other nations because of the great impact Britain, and Western Europe as whole, has made upon peoples of other lands by virtue of imperialism; and the consequences of the presence of former colonised people in Britain and Western Europe as a whole.

A remarkable feature of the United Kingdom is its 'Isles' characteristic. Like everything else, the Isles have evolved over the centuries, beginning with two isles: in c. 600 BC The Great Isle comprising England and Scotland and the Green Isle, the whole of Ireland – before the independence of southern Ireland to Post Imperial Isles in c.1900. As the name 'kingdom' suggests the United Kingdom had been ruled by absolute monarchies and later 'reigned' by a succession of kings, in fewer instances queens, by leadership amid evolving confederacies over the centuries bound up in the rich history of the United Kingdom.

The United Kingdom is made up of England, Wales, Scotland and Northern Ireland. The nomenclature 'United Kingdom of Great Britain and Northern Ireland' was adopted in 1927 and the

Church of England is an established church and a strong component in the Establishment while Parliament reigns supreme – supposedly the people ruling.

The Roman Catholic Church, mother of Christianity, has its headquarters in Rome, and since earlier times the Roman Catholic Church within Christianity had been the religious faith of the United Kingdom; though now no longer directed by Rome. Thanks to King Henry V111 who wanted to divorce Catherine of Aragon and marry Anne Boleyn but the Roman Catholic Church did not permit divorce – to this day divorce is permitted within the Catholic Church, only in some instances. He took the bull by the horns, and besides his six marriages, Henry V111 is known for his role in the separation from the Roman Catholic Church and the establishment of the Church of England, with himself as Supreme Head, a role vested in every succeeding monarch. He also achieved the union of England and Wales.

The Isle of Wight known to the ancient Romans as *Victis* is a county of England in the English Channel but is not within Great Britain. It was an independent kingdom in the fifteenth century until 1955, with a Governor, like Jersey and Guernsey; the latter two are situated off the French coast of Normandy. The Channel Islands are territories of the English Crown as successor to the Dukes of Normandy and have two main administrative units or Bailiwicks of Jersey and Guernsey. They are not part of the European Union.

An intriguing aspect of the United Kingdom is that not all the Isles share the same legal system. Scotland has its own legal system. The law of England and Wales is English common law, and its significant feature is that law is made by judges in the courts applying legal precedent to the facts before them. An Act of Parliament is primary legislation, though only Public General

Acts affect the public and apply to everyone across the entire United Kingdom. The Isle of Man's legal system is based on the principles of English common law but English law does not extend to the Isle of Man, which has the oldest parliament.

Jersey and Guernsey each has its own legal system and courts are based on common law concepts from French-Norman and English law. English common law is also the law of the Commonwealth, British Overseas Territories. The law of the United States is largely based on English Common Law, except the state of Louisiana (named after King Louis of France) which retained the French and Spanish civil law. The modern British civilisation (for want of a better word) has evolved from a variety of ancient civilisations and Britain has been a role model for her spheres of influence as other Western European powers in their own spheres and languages. Guernsey, Jersey and Isle of Man are tax havens known as `offshore banking' where investors who do not live there can invest their money to avoid paying tax in the United Kingdom. For the few who indulge in 'offshore banking', avoiding tax is not illegal but `evasion' is. Evolution may change the `avoidance' to `evasion', perhaps in pursuit of "...give unto Caesar what belongs to Caesar" but not every one is fair or a social reformer. A good number of people are endowed with the ability to amass riches and make a *difference* in the distribution of wealth through Caesar.

THE UNITED KINGDOM is a model `welfare state' and the Nordic societies come close to the UK model. In welfare, the state undertakes to protect the health and well-being of its subjects (citizens since European Union membership) particularly those in financial and social need by grants, pensions and other benefits. Unlike the rest of Europe the Nordic societies are fundamentally alike in their approach to a common set of basic values and they have a recognisable `welfare model'.

The cultural *difference* among the traditional British is great and it is not about the privileged mingling with the rest or vice versa. *Difference* in all its varieties motivates distinction in all its variety of forms and is one of the causes of poverty.

There are many categories of peers, the *exclusive syndrome,* and history has shown that exclusive is exclusion, the effect of the dogmatism of institutions, and the characteristic of the system is one that turns a blind eye to the enrichment of the rich and impoverishes the poor, the Thatcherite legacy, according to Hugo Young:

"Margaret Thatcher left a dark legacy that has still not disappeared".

The privileged and the rich in their prosaic bastion, on the one hand, and the rest on the other, regard one another with *indifference.* This is evidenced by the increase in poverty, especially among children because the poverty of any society is reflected in the standards by which children are brought up. Though United Kingdom poverty and the so-called Third World countries is incomparable, media reports indicate that it is worse than the rest of Europe, hard to believe as it may be.

2 - BRITISHNESS

Britannia, ancient Latin derived from Greek *Prettanike* or *Brettaniai,* was originally designated as a collection of islands with individual names. The Roman Empire began its conquest of the island in AD 43, established Britannia province, which survived Roman withdrawal in the fifth century. Later Britannia became Great Britain specifically. Britain was revived during the English Renaissance as a rhetorical evocation of a British national identity.

Britannia is personified by 'Lady Britannia' of the island and of martial Britannia, later used as an emblem of British imperial power and unity in the motif 'Rule Britannia', until redesigned in 2008. Towards the end of the nineteenth century, Lady Britannia was sent to the colonies, depicted on the British penny; and locally gained the name *`Cembe'*, in most Bantu languages. Hence *Cembe* came to mean `money' in the introduction of modern nexus, to a society whose method of trading exchange was barter.

Some believe that Britishness is a state or quality of being British. Prior to the late twentieth century, it may have been easier to define Britishness, but like everything else on our planet, Britishness has not escaped evolution. Imperialist consequences on infiltration and/or the absorption of exotic ideas are among the major agents of change over time.

For hundreds of years Britain has governed and protected at least a quarter of the world's people of various ethnic and cultural backgrounds. Historically, Britishness was used to refer to Britons collectively as early as 1682. After the Acts of Union 1707 between England and Scotland, the citizens of Great

Britain became distinctively separate, rather the opposite of what would be expected in a `union' – but what is in a name? There is nothing cheap about Cheapside in London, the old name for `market', the Bank of England is there.

English, Scottish, Welsh and Northern Ireland, each enjoy its own distinct culture and characteristic. Britishness was identified with Englishness but due to the novel characteristic of empire this latter identity has become blurred mainly due to miscegenation. Mixed-race people are the fastest growing ethnic group in the UK and numbered 1.2 million (2011 UK Census). Some suggest that Britishness is about shared values of tolerance, respect and fair play. Regardless of the *difference* in opinions and distinct identities most share one thing at least in common `British nationality', though some choose to ignore this factor.

`British' is nationality and British can also be attached to culture in its varying degrees. Some traditional British do not understand the meaning of the word 'British' as they tend to use it as an exclusionary device to those with a *difference* in aspect from themselves, despite that they share a common British nationality.

In granting citizenship to persons of former empires Britain had observed, to some degree, the principles of `right by blood' (*ius sanguinis*) and `right by territory' (*ius soli*) arising from control of territories that were once the `British Empire'.

Britain went beyond her shores to spread Britishness both by design and by accident, not within the entirety of the populations - a blessing in disguise, as local cultures remained intact within the majority - but those who were exposed to it, permanently altered their culture and language. A characteristic shared with other European modern empires in their foreign spheres of influence from about 1884 under the Berlin Convention. `British' is inclusive historically, and geographically embraces not only the British Isles but also former British dependencies wherever the empire spread its wings.

Ethnocentrism and class consciousness at the base of Britishness has remained immutable for centuries and is precursor to the lack of social harmony in whatever context we may look at within British society. *Difference* in its variety of forms motivates inclusion, which can also be exclusion, regardless of what that *difference* may be and is not confined to race. The phrase *ethnic minorities* points to a *difference* and is exclusionary. Every individual has a *difference,* and members of a group share a common *difference,* and the fact of *difference* applies to many varieties of differences: gender, man and woman; race, colour and somatic differences; age, young and old; child and adult; minority, varieties of groups; class and culture, language accents, lifestyle, degrees of affluence, mode of attire, etiquette; employer and employee; seller and buyer - regardless of occupation or profession where the goal is the market, or `cheapside', if you like; ruler and Ruled; and a host of others. All form exclusive groups in varying distinctive strata of supposed superiority and inferiority.

These are categorised into slots for administrative purposes; and the standard of services differ to suit the category. To this we may add other opposites: black and white; day and night; good and bad; beautiful and ugly (in the eyes of the beholder, of course!), great and small and many others.

Distinction thrives in exclusiveness, the basis of exclusion from the mainstream society which fetters freedom from the right to pursue full potential of the individual: the *archaic syndrome* and is an aspect of *benign apartheid.*

Some say that there is an identity crisis in British society to which has been added a novel situation, that of British Muslims; and that this is not caused by the strength of Islam but by the weakness of British society. Muslims as a community feel vulnerable because when a Muslim, who in fact, is a fanatic Islamist individual commits a crime, the crime is attached to the religion of Islam and all who belong to that faith. There is no such a thing as 'bad' religion or faith, only fanatic individuals make it so.

Christians have also committed serious crimes, have killed those who are not Christian, while some have killed the homosexual, albeit not in Britain in the latter. Should an entire community or religious faith be condemned for the actions of some individual fanatics? In the days of Roman rule there was no religious faith, as Christianity took hold of Europe by the sixth century CE. Britain, as other European powers, spread Christianity to the new lands, but Christianity has never removed undesirable *difference*, instead thrived in distinctions creating a number of novel *differences:* the `Roman legacy'. The root cause of this was that those who carried the Christian banner did not follow the teachings of Yeshua Mashiach, the Jew who was crucified. Instead they created their own Jesus Christ albeit 'Mashiach' (Hebrew) and 'Christ' (Greek Christos) mean the same thing: "the anointed one."

Snobbery is a form of discrimination apparent in the priority placed on the importance of 'things': starting with education, the CV, what it calls for: the type of school attended by any candidate, public and private or state schools, the latter for the children of the so-called working class since education was opened up to their children and made compulsory after the

1960s. Next comes the place of dwelling and type of accommodation: semi-detached houses on housing estates are considered superior to council houses or estates; and big houses in exclusive residential areas are seen as higher up the social ladder. Then followed by the type or the standard of cars, TV sets and modern things in technology as personal effects – all support a *difference* and a scenario of assumed superiority and inferiority.

Under organised immigration between 1850 and 1880 over three million English and Scots left Britain to populate the new Anglo-Saxon lands. Emigration was the means to address pauperism and economic imbalances in Europe, on Britain as described by John Stuart Mill:

"...the best affairs of business in which the capital of an old and wealthy country can engage."

As did other European nations in their particular spheres of interest. Where Europeans did not belong to the `upper class' in their home country, they automatically stepped into an `upper class' category in the colonised lands. In tandem with the improvement of their lives, white individuals were not only conditioned by the society in which they were born and raised but also circumstances played a part in what they had been exposed to and how they adapted to novel situations.

Like the rest of European rule of its own people in Europe based on class distinctions, transformed to "colour", in the rule of Africa and other dependencies, the basis of race and fully developed racism. Of all human *differences* pigmentation is the most obvious. In the new lands, they not only spread Christianity, but also culture and European languages. The new lands, particularly for Britain, were also convenient places to export miscreant sons.

This also created a race apart throughout European-occupied Africa, a *Mestizo* category, called *Coloured,* South African terminology, formerly *Mulatto* by the Portuguese and Spanish earlier explorers. Mixed race persons in most of Africa were stereotyped illegitimate regardless of the circumstances of their birth. Social problems arose because of the colour barrier and the illegitimate aspect. The attitudes on illegitimacy in England are well illustrated by Charles Dickens' writings, particularly, *Oliver Twist,* also highlighted by other writers. A similar situation prevailed in India since Britain's presence where mixed blood persons were called *half-caste* - what happened to the other half?

Difference was, and still is to some degree, the basis of social exclusion almost in all walks of life. Skin colour and physical traits is one influencing factor to stratification and a graded system of opportunities, by some for some, to the deprivation of the right to learn and the right to earn.

Western culture in British Africa, and other places, was influenced by many great founding persons of the Victorian era who discharged their noble duties with nineteenth-century preoccupations, much influenced by the theory of evolution. This was reflected by a succession of Victorian thinkers and writers. Contrary to the Christian concept of creation, people were conditioned to believe that peoples of Africa had not fully evolved to the stage where those holding such views had attained. On this premise, African civilisation was bypassed for centuries.

The world wallowed in old fashioned liberalism, which had followed the discoveries of Charles Darwin and other pioneers of the nineteenth century. The technology advance set the mark of civilisation and warranted European universal supremacy as the role model in Western aspects.

Reputable scholars on Africa wrote with conviction that the pageantry history of Africa remained unmoved in primitive savagery of tribal wars and absence of stable government. Yet, the monarchies of Europe rose from the ashes of tribal wars.

Missionaries were first on the African scene. As the men, white women made a great contribution to the development of the European occupied parts of Africa, and other areas. The Scots women gave education to the women of central and eastern Africa, as in other areas, and encouraged them to preserve traditional values while embracing Western civilisation. Missionaries depicted Jesus Christ on posters as a Caucasian - Yeshua, the Nazarene Jew - as sky-eyed, with golden hair. Despite that they represented Jesus who taught the `equality' of all humans, their views were no different from those of the *status quo;* and some were more prejudiced than the government administrators.

Where men liaised with local women they were shunned by their peers. They produced offspring derided by both sides of the divide. In any society, no child ever asked to be conceived - though the locals were more ready to accept such children, comparatively, the mother land as it were. The Victorian *syndrome* was an abhorrence to multiculturalism and multiracialism – sweep it under the carpet, if children could be swept under the carpet. Yet, historical records show that at least more than half per cent of the seven billion population of the world were and are conceived out of wedlock. To procreate is not always the object when two persons of the opposite sex are attracted to each other, as apparent in homosexuality, which produces no offspring, until the advent of modern technology. Despite social restrictions imposed on *culture* or *difference*, by systems of government over the centuries, individuals have defied prescriptions, transcended the barriers and mated. The mechanics of procreation, by some intrinsic but powerful reasons, are blind to *difference* of any kind, primordial to the perpetuation of the human species regardless of rank; as are other organisms that share this planet. This is a natural aspect in the 'oneness' of the human race. In the cultural but non-biological natural context, *difference* of any kind, as a barrier, is man-made.

During the Second World War British women's efforts in the Red Cross movement was significant, particularly in parts of Africa. Most of the times, before and after the Second World War, the wives of personnel wherever assigned to in Africa, played a humanitarian role amongst the local people. Not only did the men leave their names in the local populations abroad, but their names were also commemorated in roads and various structures – never those of the women, despite their honourable deeds. Skin colour and physical traits still continue to dominate people's minds across the black and white divide.

What is rife in Europe in the first quarter of the twenty-first century is political correctness by positive discrimination as some kind of an apology for past errors. A situation that creates, understandably, discontent among the indigenous persons of Europe. But perhaps the greater modern divide is between the elitist category into which leaders of non-European races have been accepted since the independence of the peoples of European empires. The category of the rest of the people is where poverty is mostly found in the majority of countries. The imbalance in social standing and wealth in the twenty-first century is unprecedented – a kind of mammon worship.

Migration is not a questionable fact of human existence since *Genesis,* because we live in one world, God's world, and colonisation or invasion is the inevitable characteristic of the power of man. African migration to Europe in recent years has accelerated to disturbing proportions, according to some thinkers. Britain over the centuries has been a bay of refuge for people of all races under various circumstances, long before colonisation of non-white races.

Now, most of Europe get their share of the influx as a result of past connections with Africa and the non-white world. The ever-running dual thread of Christian and heathen division applied to the colonial context and the development of race did not entail a complete break with earlier representation of the governed. In colonial and post-colonial contexts colour replaced class exported by the parent country but colour and class, even in modern society, have remained constant distinguishing features, albeit to a lesser degree.

The emergence of the European Convention on Human Rights in the 1950s, and the rising importance of the concept of self-determination within international law, has been a precondition to the gradual inclusion of non-white races into occupations and positions hitherto accessible to white males only. Particularly in recent times, this has been the dynamic and heterogeneous nature of prevailing circumstances, also applying to white women. Since the *Empire Windrush* docked at Tilbury on 22 June 1948, carrying a total 493 West Indian (Caribbean) passengers from Jamaica as the first immigrants to the UK after the Second World War, Britain has never been the same.

Over sixty years on, mass immigration has concentrated on England especially after the independence of colonies, importing into Britain a novel *difference,* which some view as beyond reason. Regardless of what label we may place upon it, long before Britain became an empire, her ports were open to foreigners, made up of a variety of immigrants. Some entered by occupation, others by invasion and conquest or by marriage alliances. Foreign races and cultures have infiltrated British society, from commoner to monarch. A *difference* in a low percentage of infiltration is easily absorbed into the mainstream society unlike mass immigration which rightly or wrongly, according to *difference* in opinion, is somewhat alarming.

For the most part, Britain had been ruled by non-English but rather a variety of ethnic Caucasians persons over the centuries. Some ninth-century English kings, such as Æthelstan, the half king, and Edgar, were commonly presented as rulers of Britain. The basic reason for this is that they had a loose but real leadership over the other rulers on the island – leadership is a constant recurrence in any rule but a decisive one. This leadership did not collapse in subsequent centuries, but English kings were less often described as rulers of Britain. The intensification of royal rule within the English kingdom in the second half of the tenth century made the power of kings inside the kingdom increasingly unlike their power elsewhere in Britain. Consequently it became harder to think of Britain as a single political unit. Britain has evolved through generations of different rulers of Caucasian races not all English, Scottish, Welsh or Irish, the major ethnic races as natives of Britain.

When the Roman Empire declined, Britain passed by conquest, by law, marriage, alliances, ancestral claim, or by simple accident into the hands of local war leaders; nobles and bishoprics. The Saxon kingdoms and Scandinavian invaders emerged and created regions of their own in fragmented areas what is today known as `United Kingdom'.

While `British' has remained the adjective of Britain, a historical study of the monarchy will reveal that a diverse mixture of Caucasian races, from other areas of Europe have ascended to the British throne under various circumstances, perpetuated Britain as we know it, after the Roman 400-year rule of southern Britain. The marriage of a so-called `commoner' into the royal family can be the first rung of the ladder to the British throne in a succeeding generation - social mobility of a kind. The Anglo-Saxons came in ships across the North Sea, followed by a mixture of people from north Germany, Denmark and northern Holland, Saxons, Angles, southern Danish, and Jutes, northern Danish; including a few Franks and Frisians, the German-Dutch, the Angles of southern Danish, and Jutes of northern Danish.

Perhaps of all the so-called `foreigners` who have ruled England Scotland surpasses. The recorded history of Scotland commences with the arrival of the Roman Empire in the first century CE as the province of Britannia covering England and Scotland. Scotland's ultimate victory lay in the Wars of Independence under David II which confirmed Scotland's independent sovereign kingdom, commencing with Robert II, House of Stuart, that ruled Scotland for the next three centuries uncontested.

Queen Elizabeth I of England died without children and the next in line to the throne was the reigning Stuart king of Scotland, James VI. James was a Protestant who won the backing of the English establishment and in 1567, in the union of the Scottish and English crowns, he became James I of England. Thirteen-month old baby James was crowned King James V1 of Scotland. A Scot who spoke fluent Greek, Latin, French before he could speak his native Scots, and had a different cultural background, though he was Protestant. He had sons who could succeed him, and his 36-year rule in Scotland had largely been a success. Each of the two kingdoms kept its own parliament, laws, and minted own coinage. Stuart kings and queens ruled both independent kingdoms of England and Scotland until the Act of Union of 1707 – a union that led to the dominance by England much to the chagrin of modern Scots.

The British monarchy of the twenty-first century traces its origins from the Kings of the Angles and the early Scottish Kings. The House of Anjou/Plantagenet-Angevin line produced some monarchs from 399 to 1413, and by succession of Wessex, Saxons, Germanic tribes on the North German Plain, and Anglo-Saxons. By his victory over King Harold II, last Anglo-Saxon monarch, at the Battle of Hastings in 1066, William of the House of Normandy, France, sat on the British throne. After which the Normans in Britain, forbade the English language to be spoken and imposed the French language for three hundred years. By common interest the language was preserved in secrecy. Centuries later English spoke for the world and equipped much of it with the power of words. Thereafter, an intermittent of Notables and Pretenders ruled England, followed by a Protectorate under Cromwell during the years 1649-1659, without a monarch – they beheaded their King, Charles I.

According to recorded history, establishment or entrenchment of Englishness was initiated by George V who changed the German name Saxe-Coburg Gotha, a branch of German monarchs of the Hanover Line, to the English name of Windsor (meaning "riverbank"), a situation motivated by the circumstances of the First World War with Germany.

The long reign of Elizabeth II has been the greatest ever, as she gracefully bowed to modern changes, like a solidly rooted tree whose branches take the storms; and through the smooth transition from colonial to commonwealth. Her strength and resilience comes from her mother, the last Empress of India, a position attained through her husband King Emperor of India. She was the wisdom behind the throne of her husband George VI; that of her daughter in earlier times; and as an ambassador for the Commonwealth.

How reliable are historical facts and what is truth? History taught the world to believe that King Richard III murdered the 'little princes' in the Tower of London, also confirmed by Shakespeare in his play Richard III. Josephine Tey in her book, *Daughter of Time,* presents evidence to exonerate Richard III on the ground that he had no motive for killing the little princes in the Tower, and named one who was likely to have committed the murder. Recent DNA evidence showed that the demonic portrayal of Richard was a myth, according to the sensational discovery of his remains (Guardian 27 March 2014, and other media reports). At the reburial of his bones at Leicester Cathedral on 26/03/15, a poem was read by Benedict Cumberbatch who portrayed Alan Turing in *the* film *The Imitation Game.* Both Richard III and Alan Turing shared one thing in common: they were cruelly judged, each in his own historical era.

Roman Legacy

During the early Roman Empire the *Peregrini* were free inhabitants comprising the majority. They were second class citizens commonly known as `*peregrino',* regarded as inferior to the superior Romans who were regarded as `gods'. The term *peregrini* was taken from the official term *Peregrinus* meaning `foreigner', or one from abroad' and a derivation from the adverb *peregre* `from abroad' although they were local and long standing inhabitants – a kind of syndrome (the *Roman/Peregrino syndrome*) which has contaminated people's minds since then to modern societies. Roman citizenship was granted to free inhabitants from 30 BC to 212 CE, and from 49 BC all Italians were granted Roman citizenship. From the Greek and Roman authors of classical antiquity the tendency had been to regard cultural and linguistic differences as biological differences, a thread that still runs through to the present time.

Western European scholars, conditioned by the Roman legacy of *Peregrini* from the sixteenth century onwards, sought to discover human variety in the world. Hunt, a leading anthropologist, set the trend on the theory of a hierarchy of races, which exhibited preoccupations of most nineteenth century thinkers, particularly anthropologists. This mindset reflects an upbringing in a hierarchical society of distinction, rank, wealth and privilege on one side, and the rest on the other. That everything in the world evolved from humble beginnings to a more complex state, motivated to rank their own race as above that of others. They regarded other societies as remains of extinct organisms, particularly the black people as not having fully evolved from the original state. This view was much influenced by Darwin's (1809-1882) publication *On the Origin of Species* which received the official stamp and codified as a scientific discovery – creating a major official *difference*, though a view now not widely held.

This was a *difference* that corrupted many minds over the centuries and it does crop up now and again in contemporary societies. This also fuelled, and, was directly responsible for the slave trade, perhaps the worst blemish upon Christianity.

Before the end of absolute power of the monarchy a British monarch could have been compared to a Roman emperor. The Roman Empire is the role model for Western civilisation. An aspect of the Roman legacy in Britain, until the beginning of the nineteen-eighties, was the requirement to study Latin by law students in England as a compulsory subject. According to Maine:

"There is no legal system in the world which does not contain some aspect of

Roman law."

In modern times we can trace to Roman times aspects of virtues that embrace almost our entire existence today that come under 'civilisation'; and which surpass the vices such as sophistry, snobbery and others. Since the demise of the Roman Empire, succeeding empires have been the trend setters, the role model, on the domestic scene as well as abroad, wherever they spread their rule. 'Civilisation' is an indefinable term. Murder, child abuse, and a host of other crimes and atrocities, that spell the frailty of all humankind regardless of rank, occur in the so-called civilised societies. But consider the barbaric Roman form of punishment for the accused: scourging and hanging on the cross or beam – what is the connection between civilisation and such barbarism?

Britain's characteristic of `welfare state' surpasses all other world welfare states, an aspect that could not be described as a `Roman legacy' in any manner or form.

Democracy

Democracy is a theoretical concept and the word "democracy" has it roots in the Greek language, combining two words: `*demos*' meaning  people living in a particular city-state;  and `*kratos*' meaning power, hence `people power'. Based on four principles: belief in the individual; reason and progress; social consensus; and shared power. The true meaning of democracy in practice is somewhat corrupted and there is no such a thing as total democracy. The system of some countries is more democratic than that of others. To assess the extent of democracy in any given society and its political set up, one can only make comparison between countries as to how the principle of democracy is used. Some by the two systems of election, `first pass the post' (FPTP) and `proportional representation' (PR), where they operate. What does it mean `first pass the post'? Something like a horse winning a race by being the first to reach the finishing line, usually a two-party competition. Under the FPTP system voting takes place in single-member constituencies. Voters put a cross in a box next to their favoured candidate and the candidate with the most votes in the constituency wins. All other votes `count for nothing'. Or a person is elected because he/she gets more votes than anyone else in the area that they want to represent. The weakness of this system is its competitive characteristic; and raises the question: "Who represents those whose votes count for nothing?" As Lord Hailsham put it, the system is `an elected dictatorship' – a democratic deficit. In either of any of these two systems, Prime Minister or President holds too much power, almost like a dictator. How democratic is this then?

Under the alternative system of PR, there are multi-member districts and instead of electing one person in each district several are elected – the PR is true democracy but everything depends in whose hands it is. The FPTP system is exercised in the United Kingdom House of Commons; both the United States congress chambers and the lower houses of India and Canada; the Commonwealth and others around the world. This in effect is that in FPTP countries at the top of the tree is a prime minister or a president who holds too much power and, the excessive power held by a prime minister or president leads to a big *difference* between the ruler and the ruled. Because of this *difference* not only many are left out in the cold but 'dictatorship' is absolute power and absolute power corrupts absolutely. A contemporary example is the liaison of the US President and UK Prime Minister, which led to the invasion of Iraq, without a United Nations mandate – some leaders will take people into uncharted waters. Perhaps the shortfall of democracy is that it carries the *difference* of majority and minority and in practice majority is substituted for strong while minority becomes the weak.

This administrative 'role model' extends to institutions composed of the strong: in government there is public authority – as organisations in the private sector - socially and economically omnipotent and are regulated by conventions and policies. They are represented by personnel within the bureaucracy who are vested with 'discretionary' power by delegated legislation, a logical, practical and convenient connecting device between the tree top, alienated and protected from the day to day administration; and heads of the institutions - the hierarchical system. It places order to every day life in serving the recipient of a service, the public. However, discretion is plenipotentiary, *carte blanche* to the user, the point of erosion of most individual rights: The weakest feature of bureaucracy is that at the point of erosion of a right an individual of the public is not at par with the institution's representative or agent. Where the latter has eroded a right, exclusive consideration is placed on the institution and their agents based on collectivity and a kind of 'clannish' scenario - a matter of *difference* which is indirect exclusion.

3 - ENGLISHNESS

SCOTLAND WAS ALWAYS a nation with its own national identify, legal and education system though seen as regional; civic and intellectual tradition and, of course, the kilt; and her own national flag, based on a national saint, Andrew. Wales has perpetuated its own language and culture but share a common legal and education system with England, also with her own national flag based on St David. England has her own patron saint George – if you see the St George flying at any event, be sure its a function for the "English", while the European Union tends to make the `United Kingdom' redundant. A `Common Market' was a great vision, but the addition of EC law was a travesty on domestic law – where logic ends the political reality begins! But Northern Ireland is a different story, where non-whites are more welcome than others.

GENERALLY THE ATTITUDE towards sex and food identifies the extraordinary capacity for hypocrisy in most societies. We may call hypocrisy diplomacy; deception; fiction; falsity or crudely a lie; in court a perjury; or a host of other connotations, the outcome of which may be the same but only where there is a deliberate `intention' to offend. In earlier times, the Scots, Irish (excluding the Welsh), Jews, Arabs, and the blacks, comprised the other side, had an incredible capacity for taking the mickey from the English side. One could encounter abounding jokes about the former by the English, jokes that could not be repeated in polite company, but there were very few jokes by the former to the latter. The mickeys, or jokes abound but are mere speculations on sexuality - the English are travellers in their own land – some day England shall get her independence...

The Scots and the English (not so much the Welsh or Irish) were foremost in exploring new territory before colonisation. The *difference* between them manifests itself in the mutual competitive stance they take towards each other.

When Elizabeth II is mentioned the Scots ask: "Where is Elizabeth I of Scotland?" An argument one cannot fathom. Once a reasonable English man was told, after a visit to Scotland, how green and beautiful the scenery was in Scotland, to which he replied:

"It probably rains every day there."

In all fairness, it was not only Britons held the monopoly on seed scattering, something they shared with other men universally, of those parts of the colonised world – although the Victorian *syndrome* was a clandestine attitude towards such matters. (nonetheless, apologies to the Scots and the Irish who do not wish to be called Britons! Please, do not despair, after all 'Britain' is Britannia, the Roman legacy); the German soldiers in the countries Hitler invaded, the Americans in the unpopular Viet Nam war, even the Bantu across Africa; and in older empires the Mongol empire of Genghis Khan during the thirteenth and fourteenth centuries, the largest continuous land empire that covered continents, followed by his grandson Kublai Khan; and others. All scattered their seed to make so-called 'illegitimate' children - 'little innocents' not responsible for their conception. 'Illegitimacy' is the creation of snobbery and was/is unknown in non-Western societies, where there is no such a thing as an illegitimate or an orphan child, a virtue seen by Western societies as 'wanton'; particularly under Victorian morality in attaching *difference* to legitimate and non-legitimate.

IN BUSINESS a seller may cheat a buyer, or in fields of medicine and dentistry, cheat a patient, or in other professions a client, whether diplomatic language is used, it is still pilfering because the state of equilibrium has been disturbed. There are two things that run parallel to each other in a given situation: the blatantly illegal and the softly approach. If you set upon the villain a toothless device, such as the ombudsman or a similar cudgel, it would be a much kinder retribution, by British or English standards, of course. The villain will make good and the equilibrium may be restored.   Nonetheless, "making good" under such circumstances, is a tacit admission of pilfering, regardless of the terminology employed because restoration of the equilibrium is done for self-interest: from the fear of an adverse trading record on `fitness to practice', because they have fallen into what is known as 'uninformed consent' – they always try it on the gullibility of the taker of the service.

The ombudsman and such organisations play an important role in restoring the equilibrium without resort to the courts – the British, or (particularly) English if you like, core of fairness. This situation may not arise in non-British or non-English societies because in that scenario almost everything is a `black and white' situation without gray areas. The English, the Scots, the Welsh and the Irish may each belong to their own peculiar cultures but they share a common affinity in the *pub culture* of Britishness. All types of pubs abound throughout Britain and most of the world wherever the Union Jack was hoisted. The pub is where *difference* melts and holds its own `inclusive' characteristic:

> *"I stood in the club and said 'I feel a little bored, will please*
>
> *someone take me to a pub'."*   A definition

Warmth emanates not only from the fermented cup but also

from the ambiance. In the comfort of an amiable union in the *King's Arms* or the *Queen's Arms*, therein is the cosy, recondite and well-upholstered pew for a *tete-a-tete* - but this is the jargon of yesteryear romance as the whispering of sweet-nothings.

Like everything else, pubs can be awful places when abused, though abusers are very much in the minority, if at all. The fermented cup affects some in a strange way as the *Jinni* (Genie, spirit or goblin of Arabian tales) may jump out and he will soar to a plane above those around him, like a general commanding a giant universal army. The combination of Nico and Alkie oozed out in verbal abuse sometimes extended to the bedroom – no bed of roses, romance corked in a bottle. Violence is not confined to physical abuse, nasty words is a form of violence.

At the sounding of the gong for the closing hour the *Jinni* whistles to Brandy, his dog, would walk home vociferously demeaning Brandy along the way – the dog that took the place of the wife whose heart was filled with pain and she could no longer take his abuse – poor lonely *Jinni*.

A tutor once advised a couple of foreign students to go to the pubs so they could understand British culture. A man in a pub criticised Cromwell for the state of England and asked the opinion of the two students standing next to him. Careful to avoid trouble they entirely agreed with his view, but the questioner angrily turned on them and said:

"Who are you to criticise Cromwell?"

Clubs for those who do not belong to them are a fact of *difference*. Observance of the rules of the club are the same in most groups, unwritten rules instinctively observed which perpetuates the group or the club, but not only in Englishness.

There is a merging of what is done instinctively and what governs the national aspect of our existence under the intrinsic natural rules of human behaviour.

THE ENGLISH ARE GENERALLY very polite, particularly to visitors. The landlady will look forlornly at the student setting out for college:

"I am awfully sorry, *dear*. It's raining." As if she brought the rain down. Wherever one goes the English are apologising for their weather, particularly if one comes from tropical continent, but one soon learns that weather can be an ice-breaker. Some would warn newcomers that they should not trust the three 'Ws': wine, women, and weather. The endearments are ever thrown in: dear, darling, love, etc. In the Second World War, an American in the American service based in England, thought romance was in the offing when addressed as `love' by a pretty English woman but his pal told him it was not personal. While the English said of the Americans:

"They are overpaid, over-sexed and over here."

These kind and polite endearments are also found in Scotland:

"You canee go by bus, you'rre betteer to walk, me dearre," says a kindly Scots woman to a visitor.

Northern Ireland, which remained part of Britain when southern Ireland became independent from Britain in 1922, is no less welcoming to non-white visitors. In the English scenario, the policeman taking the prisoner down says to him: "After you, Sir."

The English are always at fault never the other person. A foreign student pronounced the word `quayside' as `kweside' and received an apology from the English hostess:

"I am terribly sorry, dear. Our language is so incomprehensible."

The chauffeur sent by a host to pick up a visitor when a pedestrian suddenly run in front of the car and the chauffeur just missed running him over, the passenger said:

"That was rather silly of than man running in front of you like that, you could have knocked him over!"

"No. No. Sir, it was entirely my fault. You see, it is our duty to protect these people from themselves."

A judge at a Crown Court sentencing three men for sexually exploiting a young woman said:

"This case is a classic example of the need for the law to protect young girls from their own folly as well as from their exploitation by men."

"Stay away from the window, man. You'll catch your death of cold!" says the husband who has just found `the other man' with his wife. A non-English, or non-white husband would have shot, or speared, the other man. A woman at a cocktail party standing (usually a standing gathering) with her English companion was approached by another Englishman:

"You are lovely, very lovely. Where can I phone you?"

Not at the party, but on the way home, the companion retaliated:

"Fancy, approaching you like that in my presence! If I was not a gentleman I would have asked him outside!"

"He was bigger than you are". She replied.

"The bigger they are they heavier they fall!" He retaliated.

The motor vehicles examiner would say to the learner driver

after a driving test:

"I am afraid you haven't passed." He could just as well have said "You have failed".

Generally people tend to relegate snobbery to the upper classes but more often than not, there is snobbery in the so-called lower classes.

"There is no way I can bring my family...my grandchildren to your home", said a white Englishman who lived in a semi-detached on a housing estate, to people who lived in a council house. But it happens both ways: an Asian man residing in a council house forbade his daughter from befriending a schoolmate English lad:

"I don't want white trash from council house!"

"Don't do nothin' with my case...people who can't speak English doin' my case", said a white Englishman to a non-white English-trained lawyer volunteer assisting in a charity organisation.

In such situations, the Quakers would apply their motto of 'peace', taken from the Quran; but compare with suicide bombers who claim to be guided by the Quran, but in fact are fanatic Islamists – inter-relatedness of people, despite the *difference* in personal perception of values.

A black woman was introduced to a white Englishman fellow resident in a resident guest house.

"Where do you come from?" He asked her.

"I was born in Birmingham", she replied.

"Where did your parents come from?" He went on.

"They were both born in London", she replied.

But he was not satisfied:

"Where did your grandparents come from?".

"Look. I think you have a problem. Give us back all the treasures you took from our countries and we shall return home", she retaliated somewhat coolly.

Another tried to defuse the situation and said:

"Present anthropological evidence indicates that all humans came from Africa before they dispersed to other parts of the world."

"Not me. I am European", he went on with great conviction.

"British people are getting tired of foreigners flocking to our shores", said a white man to a non-white woman who had lived in England for thirty years, a hard-worker and tax-payer.

"Well, its pay back time", she replied. But two wrongs cannot make a right.

THE PROTECTIVE BIG BROTHER was, affectionately, called "Bobby" after Sir Robert Peel in the rallying cry:

"The Police are the Public and the Public are the Police" when he founded the Metropolitan Police - a shared responsibility. The Bobby then carried no more than a baton, if at all, but now society has evolved to the stage where some carry a gun in keeping with the type of public the Bobby has to deal with.

The American visitor asks the Bobby:

"How do I get to Lycesteer Square?"

With both his hands behind his back taking a courteous stance the Bobby politely answers:

"Lester (Leicester) Square, Sir?" Without making the questioner feel that he had mispronounced the word.

At Tottenham Court Road tube station, London, the young woman, all set for the afternoon tea dance, asks the Bobby:

"Please, can you tell me where Astoria is?"

The Bobby takes his usual courteous stance but with a touch of amusement: "Dancing, Miss?"

THE ENGLISH LANGUAGE has not escaped evolution, nor has it escaped the ever: `overt', `covet', `slanted' or the under-statement typical characteristic, "He is not a bad player", they say of the man who has just scored three goals! The Scottish equivalent of the under-statement is the word 'wee' – a wee signature (your signature somewhat alters to a 'wee' one in Scotland!), a wee while, a wee stroke, etc. There is also a side of the English language that does not reflect appropriate connotation. The dictionary translation of `paedophilia' is "sexual love directed towards children". That such cruelty to children can be referred to as '...love' is an impertinence on a beautiful language – in this respect the word `love' is corrupt. The term *straight* in the description of the heterosexual connotes the homosexual to be `bent' - the frailty of human ego in self merit. English as a language has undergone changes to remove pejorative connotations in words, for example, `cripples' in reference to those with a physical disability and the current is `physically challenged'. One hopes that the misleading `straight' will be `straightened' by evolution.

The English language has never created a social exclusionary *difference* in either pre/post-colonies, evolved to Commonwealth. In fact, it has been a unifying factor. English language was and still remains the official language of those countries in its spoken and written forms in central government and the general mode of administration. As a spoken language English was and is a second, and in a few instances third language, to the various local dialects, with the exception of persons whose parents or grandparents were born in the United Kingdom and spoke the local dialects as their second language. English is the mother tongue of India and effectively the official language of the central government. It is one of the advantages India has which is said to be propelling to economic superpower status in the growing number of parents who now aspire to give their children an education through the medium of English, the mother tongue of the elite. Given the large number of people who speak the English language in its variety of accents around the world, one may well say that English is the greatest universal *lingua franca.* Other nations learn English as part of their school curriculum but the English will not learn other languages:

"If you want to speak to me, speak to me in my language," is the attitude.

The beauty of the English language lies in its flexibility and in the absorption of foreign words and yet anchored in the rich literature of the past, the fairness of the spirit of give and take.The motivation that immigrants into the United Kingdom should have pre-knowledge of the English language as a prerequisite to residence status, the first stage in the acquisition of British nationality is unclear. One wonders about the merits or fairness of this requirement given the number of traditional Britons who do not speak grammatical English. Even some BBC presenters make grammatical errors; a common one is the split infinity of the infinitive verb `to go' which may have been influenced by the early 1980s science fiction American Star Trek film, the star ship in the Milky Way galaxy: "to boldly go..." again, the British or English fairness of give and take – the inclusion of Americanism.

Become Like Us

Generally, the majority of Britons are polite and give excessive respect to foreign cultures in their attitude that *let others be different from us.* Yet, some town councils print forms in Urdu for the convenience of Asians which is bound to retard their knowledge of the English language. Some say we will make space for you but you must become like us, whatever that means. When you do and associate with *different* others, they ask:

"And, where did you meet these people?"

The well-meaning say to the newcomer to Britain:

"You are suffering from cultural shock", and kindly advises one to watch the soaps particularly *Coronation Street* in order to become acquainted with British culture. But *Coronation Street* merely reflects one aspect of British culture – the popular. The man, who thinks he is doing her a favour, will say to his friend's lady friend (the phrase *girl/boy friend* for the geriatrics is out of place!) that she should stay at home and cook the Sunday dinner while the men go to the pub: "Remember, you are now in Britain, this is our culture!" The liberated woman would find this *archaic syndrome* patronising. As a good immigrant one must learn to fit in new surroundings; cover up one's strengths, refrain from expressing a view, hold back anger, do not excel in anything, then there might be a chance of being accepted. Otherwise one may find oneself unexpectedly kicked out of their collective imagination.

Not all incidents are bad. In fact, the bad ones are few and one may come across many pleasant ones of comparatively overwhelming racial/cultural harmony besides inter-marriage. Here is one that would lift the spirits. In a northern city a white English woman was pushing an Asian woman in a wheelchair. Speaking to strangers is very un-British or un-English, if you like. The English woman's daughter had married the son of the Asian woman. The two ladies went on about their three beautiful common grand children.

One of the greatest virtues of British society is tolerance and the fundamental basis of the law is to protect all equally. The home of free speech is the soap box in London's Hyde Park, Speakers' Corner, where all forms of free speech must not be interrupted. One particular Sunday morning, a German speaker was on the soap box running down the English and praising the Scots as outstanding `British' trail blazers in colonisation, as in other things: a Scotsman would blaze the trail, an Englishman would follow, hoist the Union Jack and take the credit. Then the speaker says to the audience: "Those of you who are English put your hands up!" Only one hand comes up – a black man's hand!

KARL MARX, a German immigrant, made a great contribution to the good of the United Kingdom in his slogan: "Workers Unite"; as many other immigrants in many fields, from commoner to monarch – the beauty of Britain is that foreign infiltrations, in all its idiosyncrasies, prevails. But compare, from the last decade of the twentieth century, take a flight from any Western European city headed for Africa and one would be intrigued to find that almost every seat on the plane is occupied by white males heading for Nairobi, Kenya, the central point on the African Continent and gateway to the world - to connect flights. Mostly to African cities or various non European countries, for business and employment and a very small percentage of travellers are tourists.

If all the traditional British and other Europeans (including Eastern Europe), who live and work in foreign countries, were to be repatriated to Britain and the others to their respective countries, could their native countries sustain them? Migration exchange is a contemporary norm and inevitable in human existence.

Self Exclusion

Groups are exclusive and are not only exclusionary to others but also lead to self-exclusion because they create a *difference* between themselves and the host country. Those immigrants who choose to cling to their own culture, and make no attempt to learn the language of their adopted country, and put their original tradition in second place, take the risk of self-exclusion from the main-stream society.

In the field of entertainment or the performing arts, particularly the pop groups, the younger people appear to be more at home in multicultural and multiracial societgies. Examples of self-exclusion situations are evident in the United States: to be known as `African-American' by choice, is self-exclusion from mainstream `American' society. Though one thing is significant: `African American' embraces not only black people but also those who are of `mixed' descent. Obama is hailed not only by Africa but also by the whole world as the first `black' man to occupy the White House as President of the United States but in fact, he is of mixed races.

In the United Kingdom nationality is `British' inclusive of all those who hold British nationality subject to certain qualifications to obtain national status, but do any of these factors minimise racial problems?

The Jews are in a similar situation anywhere. They have over the centuries remained a distinctive group from mainstream society pursuing their beliefs and values. By remaining a distinct group is self-exclusion. They have also intermarried into other societies as can be seen by the *difference* in ethnicity within the Jewish faith. Nonetheless, people should be free to choose to belong to a particular faith or group and that should not be a reason to exclude them from mainstream society.

Almost in every country of the world there are ethnic groups and it well becomes most of us to celebrate the *difference.* Although England is a highly class conscious culture they way a person's position is determined in the class structure bears little relation to the so-called three-tier upper, middle and lower models and may be assessed by the way they do things. There is no place like England where common nationals are so diverse in their outlook, yet each know their place in society until an alien or `foreigner', as the Britons call them, comes in their midst and their common differences dwindle.

4 - CLASS AND CULTURE

Class and culture is more particularly in reference to possessions, beginning with the type of house and location, cars, clothes, food, clubs one belongs to, type of education, and others. The English language, is an expressive and descriptive language, to the extent of derision, and varies according to the class to which a person belongs: harlot is a Biblical term; courtesan or call girl is upper class; and prostitute is general. All share one thing in common promiscuity in a form of earning for existence, much derided in most societies, but in fact, is an occupation that should call for compassion. Who is to define sin? We are all sinners in the *difference* of definition.

Class and culture is a situation that constantly evolves and perhaps the way to describe it might be: `from clogs to riches to clogs'. Class and culture is exclusive, hence exclusion. A `classless society' is a myth. Class is a historical, reality and a questionable factor contemporary at its own making irrelevant to race. Class is created by the accident of human relations static or migrant. An individual becomes a member of a class by playing a social role important in the capacity of authority in relation to influential expectations; more often than not by accident of birth, or infiltration by choice aided by the lucre, education, or marriage. The basis of class is *difference* in legitimate power affiliated to certain positions.

Some believe that Marxism influenced a classless society but it merely sped members of the so-called `lower' classes to the middle class by the lucre, in successful profitable enterprise. Some aspire through education and politics. Class and culture has always been a topical area of sociology and has evolved with time only to its characteristic. In recent times political correctness refrains from usage of the terminology `class', a form of hypocrisy, because class distinctions have remained immutable for centuries to the present. Also mimicked by those who are at the tree top in the areas wherever Western European flags were hoisted.

Class-consciousness is the way in which the incidence is viewed in cultural terms. Therefore, class and position is derived from the benefice of a social role; and the *class distinctions* of British society is the immutable *status quo*. If class is a distinction that divides the traditional British nation in the *status quo* of British society one may well ask: what is the place for the so-called ethnic minorities? Distinction highlights *difference,* is exclusion, and a form of discrimination and consequently *benign apartheid* exercised by people as opposed to government policy in some instances.

There is little in common between the privileged and the rest and the *difference* in culture is as cheese from chalk, although they share a common nationality, domicile and a common sense of belonging. The traditional, as opposed to the *nouveau riche,* privileged may be distinguished by the significant *difference* in lifestyle and usage of the English language: vocabulary, humour and accents; and a good pointer is how `tea' is served.The upper class drink tea and not eat it as the main meal of the so-called working class, particularly in the north. Tea has been such a popular drink since colonisation and very much a part of British culture and a rather intriguing fact of life.

Regardless of status peoples of the former colonised areas `drink' tea and do not eat it, to this day, the Victorian role model. Tea is a colonial commodity which much characterises Britishness. Offer an Englishman a cup of tea and he will answer in the affirmative in a particular kind of jargon:

"Can a duck swim?"

"Now, you are talking!"

"What did the cup say to the teapot?

"There is nothing I'd like better", and many others.

Offer a Scotsman a cup of tea and he will say:

"I'll neever say Noo."

Due to primarily climatic conditions, and economic reasons, tea was never and could never be grown in the British Isles. Every stage of tea production is a subject of slave labour which brought and still brings much wealth to the planters, agents and others engaged in the production of tea at the tree top. The agricultural workers in the tea fields work from dawn to dusk for a pittance. Even under new black leaders in the tea growing areas, after their independence from Britain and in some instances Western Europe, the situation has changed little to this day.

The second pointer is that the traditional upper class add `sauce' to a dish while the popular class add `gravy.' The high class enjoy the blessings of privilege and few suffer pecuniary embarrassment and their affluence is apparent not by vaunt. They perpetuate the Old World and English, or sometimes termed as British, cultural values, mellowed as a liqueur brandy, little touched by novel exotic infiltrations. Though the Indian `samosa' and the Mexican `chilli con carne' has captured their palate, as an occasional treat, quite a feat from the cold Victorian cucumber sandwich.

The *nouveau riche* would be desolate in their midst. Likewise, the privileged would be equally disorientated within the latter scenario. Money does not make a fool of anyone it only shows them up and, for some, it can buy snobbery.

Prior to the twenty-first century, the upper class were mostly white hardly any non-white, and were predominantly British or English, now they include a few from other races. Since the English and the Scots are great sailors a few married on their foreign travels and brought home the darker races and their offspring assimilated into the mainstream white society particularly by the third generation.

Along with the cultural division of the privileged and the rest is the *difference* in the standard and quality of public facilities and amenities in almost every field, down to the standard of road repairs – in the southern cities of the privileged one hardly ever encounters portholes. The rest in its historical development at the ground level is the popular strata comprising manual workers in towns and countryside – the so-called `working class' - an abhorrent phrase, as if they worked without using the brain. They gained the position of power that could bring industry to a grinding halt by and since the Marxist ideology: `Workers Unite' in the rise of trade unionism. A power shattered by Thatcherism.

Arising from the same ideology was the first strata of an upstart group, plain, simple with recently acquired ostentatious wealth and middle-class ideas, the *bourgeoisie* also known as the *nouveau riche* of modern times. Both the popular and the latter were white, at a time when race was irrelevant until the movement of people from non-white areas; although sharing a common British nationality, they had little else in common and the *difference* was mainly cultural.

The traditional ruling class, in a secular extended sense of the original established Church of England, was composed of a variety of middle and upper classes: the Crown, now the powers of the Crown are exercised by a prime minister, and the saving grace for the survival of the British monarchy, when other monarchies of Europe were crumbling, was the status of `constitutional' monarchy.

Charles II died in 1685 without an heir and his brother became King James II. He was removed in 1689 by parliament because he was as tyrannical as his father, Charles I who was beheaded. Parliament asked James' daughter Mary II and her husband William of Orange to become King and Queen. Executive power and powers over taxation were given to parliament, leaving the monarch as a figurehead, so ended absolute monarchy; and Britain became a constitutional monarchy.

THE MONARCHY WAS BASED on a 300-plus-year old piece of discriminatory legislation, whereby access to the throne was denied to female successors where there were male heirs, regardless of female seniority by age; and to Catholics, and other non-Protestants. A fact of *difference* in the monarchy is that the wife of a king is accorded the status of 'queen' and carries the title `her majesty'; whereas the husband of a queen is not accorded similar status. There have been proposals that the discriminatory legislation governing the monarchy on accession should be amended for eldest child to be heir to the throne regardless of gender. This was implemented in <u>2013</u> to affect those born after 28 October 2011 (Perth Agreement, Western Australia, by 16 prime ministers of 16 Commonwealth realms). Some have suggested that by the same token, it would be good to see that the wife of a king is accorded the status of `consort' rather than queen, to balance the *difference* from that of the husband of a female monarch, who cannot be called 'king'.

After the monarchy in the order of precedence were the Court; the aristocracy; the Church; the judicature; the senior civil servants; Oxbridge; the General staff; the City; heads of the banking world and industry; and the big corporations. These divided into two English or British classes: upper class, best described as the *privileged* class, a `cosy Club', dividing them from all the rest in the *status quo*, which has since evolved only by its characteristic, such as immigration from other lands and the Commonwealth. Since 1914 the upper class became superimposed on one another through significant qualifying elements within their closed cosy club converging from three streams: the *aristocrats,* the *plutocrats* and the meritocrats. Aristocrats consisted of families having wealth and power based on landed property, whose influence declined but not prestige. Plutocrats were the ruling wealthy ascended through Victorian and Edwardian eras, heads of industry and trade, through matrimony, finance, politics and alliance with the aristocrats; and the Meritocrats, selected according to merit, who derived power from their expertise.

Mingling of these latter three streams formed the Establishment, exclusive to the rest manifest in dogmatic institutions – the mother of institutionalised "class", which has survived resentment of the strong among the rest, and has held its own at the apex of state and society.

In recent years there had been an attack on the House of Lords by the House of Commons in the proposed changes for an elected chamber. Adaptation to contemporary society may be inevitable for the survival of institutions, provided that such changes are proposed for the common good and not in favour of the group that proposes them – but sadly, some changes are proposed for self-interest. The irony to this proposal is that now more and more peerages are given to people, hitherto unthinkable that they would be accorded such, for `political correctness'.

MARXISM SET THE ROLE MODEL for subsequent pressure on the *status quo* hitherto unquestioned. Social change, like class, is the accident of human relations and is a historical questionable happening contemporary at its own making. The Marxist conception of class and power politics was a redefinition of class which was the vehicle to the middle class by the *nouveau riche* and leaders of former dependencies as a novel addition to the pre-existing classes. In reality it was the unfolding of ideals in the dissentience to paternalistic protection and its inevitable consequences which were not always surmountable.

The pressure on the *status quo* manifested in the late 1950's-early 1960s, in feminism and in the principle of self-determination backed by the European Convention on Human Rights. Along with the 1960s changes in UK was the availability of education to the rest.

The consequence of the migration fleeing from a provenance beset with problems of self-determination gone awry, has had its impact on European society, particularly British society, because of its welcoming shores comparatively, economically, and culturally, not to mention the inter-mingling of genes.

Racism has become unlawful and yet in manner of all administration persons are referred to in racial terms by the phrase *ethnic minorities*, sometimes a phrase often used when positive discrimination is being exercised for political correctness.

5 - RACE AND RACISM

RACISM WAS A NOTION that human abilities were determined by race. The notion of `race' had dominated most societies on Earth over the centuries. The object of both creation and evolution bear the basic humanitarian attributes but neither creation nor evolution has been free from racism. Some choose to use religion or science to their own ends. From the Greek and Roman authors of classical antiquity to the present, the tendency had been to regard cultural and linguistic differences as biological differences. European scholars, particularly from the sixteenth century onwards, sought to discover human variety in the world. Attributes of somatic differences, particularly colour, gave way to mutual assessment for the formulation of functional strategy and this led to evaluation of unreal beliefs of what was assessed, and consequently the categorisation of people. Environmental and climatic conditions also influence characteristic traits. Upon the multiplication of milliards emerged racial classification.

Some more equal than others. Lienhadt quoted Hunts' theory of a hierarchy of races as exhibiting very crudely a nineteenth century preoccupation of anthropologists. Other thinkers reflected their upbringing in a hierarchical society distinction, rank, wealth and privilege. They regarded other societies as the fossilised remains of those extinct organisms from which evidence of human evolution was taken. This view was much influenced by Darwin's publication of *On the Origin of Species* which was interpreted as a demonstration of everything in the world having evolved from humble beginnings to a more complex state. The idea that humankind is divided into races was codified and given an apparently 'scientific' stamp by intellectual thought of the nineteenth century. Now less widely held but it is still more prevalent than it deserves. At a stage of the world competing for imperial powers belonging to the best race was very important – they could not connect or distinguish the difference between 'physical evolution' and 'social evolution'.

Towards the end of the nineteenth century Durkheim and colleagues proposed a more considered science of society than earlier exponents. Durkheim believed that the individual's conscience was moulded by social tradition. That different societies exhibit different patterns of thought and view other societies according to their own learned classification of things. Linneaus' classification of species, though prior to Durkheim and his contemporaries, was that it was logical to arrange animals in accordance with their analogous characteristics. Under contemporary science classification of animals was based on their genetic affinity, in other words divided into species. It was not until David Attenborough emerged that, those who have not lived with and studied animals, are able to understand the 'true' nature of animals and wildlife on our planet. Attenborough has given the world a 'holistic' insight into animal life: from birth to adulthood, their mating habits, social organisation, how they care for the young and other values.

In colonial and post-colonial contexts emphasis of colour and cultural characteristics had remained constant distinguishing features as the established *status quo.* In Britain many academic authorities would be prepared to say that 'races do not exist' but why are there statutory bodies concerned with race relations? In the same way there are organisations such as the Society for the Prevention of Cruelty to Children (SPCC), Royal Society for the Prevention of Cruelty to Animals (RSPCA), and trade unions, because cruelty to children and animals, and iniquitous conditions of employment respectively, existed and still exist.

One of the remarkable things about Britain is the charitable stance of the people of traditional Britain. Besides the above charities there were, and still are, many other charities which serve as a 'safety net' for those in need of some service which they cannot afford for lack of knowledge, or lack of resources. And, the kindness and compassion with which charity workers dispense services to those in need in Great Britain, are second to none. It has also been said that 'charity' is big business in Britain and some of those at the top of charities get exorbitant salaries, and live well above those in the lower echelons. A universal characteristic in almost every institution that dispense services to the public.

Skin colour is an extremely trivial characteristic of importance to human physiology, not permanently associated with any other physical or cultural features; and it is of no moral or scientific value. Because skin colour is very visible, it is the most common *difference* upon which comment, inclusion or exclusion is made. The mono-genesis of Caucasian races suffered and still suffer less racial derision because of the absence of obvious pigmentation as manifested in the poly-genesis of Caucasian, Asian, and Black races. Historical records show that the characteristic of our existence over the centuries has been over shadowed by those who have used religion or science to focus on *difference* as a means to exclude others for their own ends influenced by pre-conceived ideas. In the preoccupations of the nineteenth century, the concept of "Darkest Africa" had been referred to as the "Victorian image of Africa" - as if Africa needed electric light. Confirmed and regarded as the norm rather than corrected and modified. "...that some men were born slaves was a natural state of Affairs", so said Aristotle.

There are two aspects to `evolution', biological and cultural, but most believe that it is not as perceived by Darwin. True evolution may be seen in the biological aspect: we all begin as a dot from the sperm and evolve through incubation, birth to a fully grown adult, beyond to old age and after death in the stages of decay. On the cultural aspect, no baby is born with a culture of any kind. Babies are always mimicking what they see others doing around them, who influence the tender mind in understanding the world. The administration of our contemporary institutions, whether private or government, is based on the Roman hierarchical model though as outdated as the division of species. Those at the top are `Roman' and regard those in the lower echelons as *Peregrini* and less deserving. This is apparent in today's unprecedented redundancies almost in every organisation or institution, be it government or private and this is not done in racist terms.

Perhaps some of the most contentious issues in race relations had been debated in the United States. One matter, particularly concerned the derivation of cultural qualities from biological difference, was that of intelligence, and this was of common assumption, among whites in the USA. Some may recall how racially diverse `whites' were once thought to be: that blacks had lower intelligence, because they came from an inferior race, though this attitude was not confined to the USA. A view strongly contested, as part of a general re-valuation of the place of the blacks in American society; and studies purported to show that in objective intelligence tests, blacks performed systematically less well than whites. Some took this as confirmation of what they had always known.

Others argued that the blacks were the product of systematic cultural deprivation, and so could not be expected to perform as well as the privileged whites. The difference was one of cultural conditioning, not heredity. Racism in Europe has not been anti-black but anti-Semitic (Biblically Semite, descendant of Shem, son of Noah). They belonged to a self-defining religious group, also in biological terms over many generations. There was a *difference,* a big difference, from the mainstream society. The demonic actions of Hitler was notorious to the ends of the world. In the remotest villages of Africa where they spoke no other language but their own dialects, when a boy misbehaved the parent would say:

"Who do you think you are, Hitler?"

It was a *difference* which would disappear once the cause was removed, but since there is no measure for effects of biological heredity the problem may remain.

A baby in the womb can be influenced by the lifestyle of the parents, such as HIV contacted within the womb, particularly in deprived societies. Once born the child is already a member of a particular culture, benefiting from its strengths and retarded by its weaknesses. Racial differences are created by societies, a general human tendency to attribute human differences to biological origins and to rank one's own race as above that of others. Humans tend to group themselves together according to race, religion, country of origin or other common similarities, because it is easier to live with or survive within it. Some groups are self-defining in biological terms and groups become physically distinguishable from the majority population; thus are more easily vulnerable to racial, religious or other preoccupations.

Racism indicates a *difference* that finds expression in a mutual mediation between human beings, and colour is a constant variable distinguishing feature while class is associated with position in tandem with the nature of culture.

From the nineteenth century in the areas of imperial influence, race was used as a social exclusionary factor against the non-white races, while the white race was a prerequisite to social inclusion in all aspects: availability of jobs, social services and a host of other things necessary for the dignity of human existence.

Large scale migration has the tendency to invoke debate about 'race'. The migration of different European peoples to the North American continent led to endless debate about the racial characteristics and its worth. For example, the races: Irish, English, Italian, Scottish, German, Polish, and so on, and the migration of European troops, administrators, traders, and to other parts of the world during the colonial period. The latter led to the original formulation of the theories of race discussed above; the return of people from the colonised countries to the colonising country, in search of work was another, leading to British and French pre-occupation with racial problems; the general migration of people to find work was another, to the large presence of Turks in West Germany and Italians in Switzerland; the forced migration through the enslavement of many Africans from the west and east coasts of the African continent to the American continent, was another.

Perhaps no other place was like South Africa where there had been the social questionable reality commonly known as `passing' was so true. During the apartheid regime of South Africa: those who were `white' could pass the legal colour barrier known as `colour bar', despite their black origins - there are those in every historical era who will try to cheat the contemporary system. Other than the tribal inhabitants found in South Africa by the white migrants as labourers and slaves, the

East India Company imported, those then called Negroes, from parts of tropical Africa. In some cultures it was acceptable to own slaves and the slave population increasingly acquired Caucasian genes. The mingling of genes between white male colonists and transients, slaves, and Khoikhoi women was common in South Africa. The light skinned passed as "whites" and crossed the colour bar into the white community, the basis of apartheid. People mixed genetically but never socially throughout white-ruled Africa. Generally the offspring inherited the mothers' status and joined the mixed communities of displaced Khoikhoi, escaped slaves and vagabond whites disdainfully called "Bastaards", later termed Griquas (South Africa).

In the Shire Highlands, present day Malawi, the number of mixed blood persons was insignificant in terms of population until organised European immigration in the latter part of the nineteenth century and the beginning of the twentieth-century. The practice was by no means confined to South Africa. European empires governed by double standards: in the mother country `class' and in the colonies `colour' throughout the Empire. Most people have been so indoctrinated by this kind of thinking because the imperial rulers were the trend setters and the role model for the locals. In the mid-1990 in Scotland a Scottish young woman referred to two certain young women, and those around, failed to place them because she had referred to them as `Scottish'. When she pointed them out, then it was realised who they were: born in Scotland of Asian parents from South Africa. Such is the entrenchment of 'race' in the conditioning of the minds of people.

In South Africa, what was called 'separate development' of peoples, and separateness became a way of life to the extent where, despite the end of apartheid, people stick to their own racial groups. There is no inter-mingling of the races, in the twenty-first century, the power of conditioning. In the 'end of apartheid' we have a shining example of the power of Time which brought us to the heretofore unimaginable milestone. A 'black' person, and a 'woman' at that, was the judge in the murder case of a white man, Oscar Pistorius, for the killing of his girlfriend – the sad end of a paralympic athlete Olympic hero – a champion runner without legs. During the apartheid era, the highest position a black woman could aspire to was nanny/domestic servant in a white household.

In Malawi, once they got over "the boot is on the other foot" period after independence - in the resentment and cruelty directed at non-black people - had something to tell the world: no race or colour barriers and people mixed and socialised freely, as a way of life. But currently there are signs of discrimination and tribalism – the inevitable aspect of evolution. It is no longer fashionable to exclude the consequences of racial difference in modern Europe, migration results in inter-mating, and the emergence of new racial groups. If we are to base the debate on science, then we would look to the role genes play: humans do not know what gene mixtures they carry in their bodies.

ONE ASPECT of the role played by genes is migration, which is based on inter-mating, and the emergence of new racial groups. But if one contrasts two scenarios: the poly-genesis of black and white races may be dominated by mono-genesis within generations, even as few as three: a black mono-genesis over a number of generations would produce black offspring, as would the product of white where there was white mono-genesis, produce white offspring. Once within the mono-genesis mainstream society, the black or white *difference* dissipates and becomes insignificant: because it is not obvious to the naked eye. Climatic and environmental conditions also influence characteristic traits. But the most important aspect of this debate is that after several generations, there has been and there can be a throwback: black in the white or vice versa.

In Malindi, on the East Coast of Africa, the Swahili emerged, a people and language of the same name. They were a race apart by the liaison of Arabs and local black women, in the fourth century CE. The Arabs, unlike white men, were more ready to recognise their offspring by black women, educated them in the Arab culture and Islamic religion.

The Swahili were disdainful of their less privileged cousins, became a powerful clan in the area and engaged in international trade in ivory, other commodities, and later were at the forefront of the `slave trade' in their area. At some point in time of history, the Swahili became integrated into and within mainstream society, and as a group of people dissipated. Swahili became the official language of Kenya and Tanzania, besides English and other vernacular languages.

Since the dawn of time in all nations, even the Communist regime of Russia, which promised equality for all when they murdered their royal family: there has always been the elite and privileged above, the head within the hierarchy, and a wide gap down to rock bottom in varying degrees, where the rest were and still are, the tail. Though the Russian scenario was independent of the *Peregrini* syndrome label. We are now in the twenty-first century has this situation changed?

Maybe the change is no so visible, and only as to its characteristic. In fact, this is the tragedy of Africa and other developing countries: those at the top mimic the elite of developed nations in lifestyle and everything they do but without a welfare aspect of governing and reserves in the treasury. While some take chemicals to lighten their skin: the *Michael Jackson syndrome.* When they say there is much poverty in developing countries, the question is who is poor in such or any country where there is poverty?

Racism now is abhorred particularly since the post-war immigration from the new Commonwealth to Britain, especially from the Indian sub-continent and the Caribbean, but it still exists among a few who can create ugly situations. And, this is not confined to white against non-white but also vice versa.

Over the centuries Britain's ports have been an open door to persons of different nationalities who, for a variety of reasons, sought refugee in Britain. Until the post war migration most of the immigrants into Britain were of European origin. Because there was no genetic *difference*, in particular skin colour and their culture was not so dissimilar to those of the peoples of the host country, and a common Christian religion, the question of `colour' never arose as that of post independence immigrants. Hence, there were few or no reports on racist incidents. The newcomers were more easily assimilated into the host communities; though they grouped themselves according to country of origin: Italians, Greeks and others, particularly in London, as humans normally do wherever they are.

Many societies of the non-Western world were and are still organised under a kinship structure where relationships of kindred are greatly extended to include very large numbers of people. Their kinship is fundamental to their social organisation. Many societies in the Western world have within them very elaborate systems of ranking which are expressed in terms of biological exclusiveness and hierarchy; particularly so for the 'jewel in the crown' of the British Empire, India, within its caste system. European imperialism used racialism to justify its activities but most of those societies which it governed were as 'racialist' as the governor - they just didn't have the might of industrial expertise behind them. Physical and social anthropologists, geneticists, and human biologists and scholars of humanity in general are now mostly united in rejecting the idea of race. The notion that all humans are, at the physiological and biochemical level, and that the differences are minimal, prevails today. And leading to the conception of having one human race only.

Absolute equality is impossible because of the *difference* in the uniqueness of perception of each individual. But the gap between the rich/privileged and the rest is great and this is the big question of the twenty-first century. Individuals are conditioned not only by the society in which they are born and raised but also historical and universal circumstances play a part in what they have been exposed to and how they adapt or react to it, particularly migration. In Britain for example, particularly in recent times, the dynamic and heterogeneous nature of prevailing circumstances has been a precondition of the gradual inclusion of non-white races into occupations and positions hitherto accessible only to male of the white race. In the contemporary context the term 'racism' is incorrectly applied save for a small percentage of situations where racism is an ugly reality. Particularly social exclusion which leads to unequal treatment in employment or the availability of employment - a situation which is focused upon a kind of *difference*.

ETHNOCENTRISM in eastern central Africa was almost identical to that of South Africa, except in the latter segregation was controlled by statute. Nonetheless, this raises the question: What is the difference between legislated and non legislated discrimination if the outcome is the same? Religious worship (Mostly Christian, Islam and other minority beliefs) was integrated in eastern central Africa unlike South Africa.

An example of the South African scenario explains the nature of segregation. A black employee cleaner in a church for whites was told by a white worshiper: "God help you, if I catch you praying in here…" Nonethess, imperial-exported Christianity in Western European colonised areas, was seeped in elitism far beyond the understanding of ordinary people.

It is said that though Barack Obama travels on Air Force One, his children cannot swim in pools for 'whites'. Perhaps we could put this down to the exclusiveness in the bastion of private social clubs. In any event, exclusiveness is exclusion.

The African Negro (a pejorative term no longer popularly accepted) had been depicted as void of any history but Medieval Africa held civilisations and societies as vivid as those of medieval Europe. Some say by European lack of appreciation of Arab literature and records, the opportunity to pay due regard to the natural virtues of Africa was lost to the world. However, this is debatable.

One may ponder on the absence of great ancient monuments in Africa, such as the Zimbabwe Ruins. The bronze statue of Cecil Rhodes at the top of and looking down Jameson Avenue in Salisbury, now Harare, was obliterated to the very foundation by order of Robert Mugabe. Rhodes was a great empire builder who built a railway system from Cape to Cairo, also by Britain in eastern and central Africa, now all gone to wrack and ruin since the independence of African countries.

North Africans such as Pharaoh Tuthmosis 111, Sesotris 1, Narmer, or Menes and the Spinx populated and started the ancient civilisation of Egypt. Herodotus, the Greek historian in four hundred BC, described Egypt as black:

> *"These people, these Negroes (for neat racial pigeon-holes have little application here) undoubtedly multiplied in the years after about 5000 BC. An analysis of some 800 skulls from pre-dynastic Egypt from the lower valley of the Nile, that is, before about 3000 BC shows that at least a third of them were Negroes or ancestors of the Negroes whom we know; and this may well support the view, to which a study of the Africans of today were important and perhaps dominant element among populations which fathered the civilisation of ancient Egypt -* Davidson.

Hollywood has produced most exquisite and inspiring films of 'white' players/actors portraying the Queens and Pharaohs of Egypt in their most fascinating existence in an ancient civilisation (as most civilisations) built on slave labour. In school history curriculum the world was conditioned to believe that Egypt was not in Africa because they could not attribute `civilisation' to black people. Likewise, American cowboy films exclude black cowboys though they existed. (Modern producers do not appear to make cowboy films any more.) Only in recent times has Egypt been acknowleddged as situated in Africa, bordered by the Mediterranean sea to the north, by Western thought and that its advancement from the Fourth to the First Millennium BC was a local precept of the Nile Valley motivated by Negro (as they were called then) and Asian races. This was previously attributed to Greek and Roman contact with Egypt. African art had been ignored for centuries. In the former Western European power and the novel African power, the leaders of each could not gap the *difference* between them, audacious in their own era. The magnificent bronzes of Ife dating back from the thirteenth-century were not assessed and appreciated until 1938; the beautiful bronzes and ivories of Benin were discovered and appreciated in 1897; and the stone remains of Great Zimbabwe in 1868. The list goes on. Exquisite works of art by the African throughout modern Africa today, reflect traces of ancient artistic skills.

FLORENCE NIGHTINGALE (dob 12/05/1820, Florence, Italy) was the daughter of wealthy English parents who were on tour in Italy when she was born. She was an outstanding woman who established nursing as a respectable profession for unmarried women (in the spinning wheel days). She became famous for her work in the military hospitals during the Crimean War. Her parents considered nursing to be a profession not suitable for a woman of her class and background, and forbade her to train as a nurse. They expected her to enter the 'respectable' role for a woman: good marriage and a conventional upper class woman's life.

Mary Jane Grant (later Mrs Seacole, born 1805, Kingston, Jamaica), a slave, her fame rivalled Florence Nightingale's during the Crimean War. She travelled much and arrived in London to offer herself as a volunteer nurse in the war but she was met with racism and refusal. Undaunted and independently, she set out to the Crimea, where she was doctor and 'mother' to wounded soldiers while running her business, the 'British Hotel'. Her story gives an insight into the history of race politics. The cause of the Crimean War (1853-February 1856) was about the rights of Christian minorities in the Holy Land, which was controlled by the Ottoman Empire; a conflict in which Russia lost to the alliance of France, Britain, the Ottoman Empire, and Sardinia.

EXAMPLES OF MINORITY and ethnocentrism in reverse are decolonisation of African countries. Similarly, Russia had acquired, and settled in a number of territories, in the Baltics known as the 'titular states'. In the West, the Berlin Conference of 1884-85, the international instrument to divide Africa geographically among Western European powers, was Africa's undoing in more ways than one. By the time of independence for Africa beginning in the 1950s, the continent had acquired a legacy of irreparable political factions as set by European colonising powers. Each African leader posed as a big fish in a small pond, without the already laid on railway communication between the new African states.

After the decolonisation of Africa, the tables turned. The white minority lost dominance because they no longer belonged to the ruling race in those parts of the world. In the Russian example, in Estonia the requirement to learn the Estonian language as a prerequisite to the acquisition of citizenship presented a dilemma for the Russian minority. This was retaliatory to the former Russian imperialist policy of mandatory acculturation to the Russian language as an integration device to what was called `russification'.

In both the central African and Russian situations was that persons of a privileged status found themselves subordinated, excluded from the socio-cultural, political and economic life and shared a common citizenship problem, without the right to equal opportunities. Race and minority combined to form a potential *difference* and became the exclusionary factor. Rather, the problem of culture was conditioned by sociological norms. Other similarities included organisational methods modelled on that of the outgoing power and the recognition of a two-tier ethnic society. In the central eastern African example animosity was directed at the white and Asian minorities who were not nationals of the new nation in the process of Africanisation. Throughout the centuries, from an old to a new era, there is the transitional period, in which are individuals or groups who pay the price of transition, caught between two stools as it were. Leaders of newly independent Africa, reacted in various ways: some more cruel than the regimes they replaced, in the attitude of 'the boot is on the other foot' where the white and Asian minorities were concerned, were held responsible for the actions of their ancestors.

The generation of the twenty-first century are awed in disbelief when told that, in the past one could travel over two thousand miles by train; through Mozambique, Zimbabwe, and on to South Africa, from Livingstone's Nyasaland (Malawi), and on to Cairo - the railway system that is no more. In Europe, not only the monuments and works in the structures of the past are appreciated and preserved in history, but also personages connected with them in all their aspects – warts and all.

In the Tanzania of the twenty-first century, the local people make up of one hundred tribes each with its own dialect; Arabs; Asians, predominantly Indians brought in by Britain in the 1880s to build the railway; Eastern and Western Europeans; Africans from neighbouring countries; and other minorities. All combined and evolved into a common culture of 'Umoja' - 'oneness' of the nation - vision of the leader Julius Nyerere.People exist within different levels of affluence where the wealthy vaunt not their riches; they share a common diet, a concoction of world cuisines; and the racial harmony is second to none. The country is economically sound and free from the dictates of donor nations (2014 CE). However, soon after independence from Britain, the Asian women paid the price for "Umoja". They were forced to marry black Tanzanian men, to create 'the oneness' of the nation. The women became utterly lost, with a 'vacant' look in their eyes, they walked like zombies. It has always been easy for men to marry into other cultures over the centuries but not for women. The offspring of this union, several generations on into the twenty-first century, walk about with the same 'vacant' look, resigned to their fate in complacency.

Before the independence of Africa from European empires, forced marriages were common among mixed Asian, African, and European Westernised societies, both Christian and Moslem. The female child was regarded as a burden and unwanted: the *difference* of gender. In Uganda, Idi Amin took the cake. Most African leaders disregarded Biblical New Testament tenets despite their claim to the Christian faith. But contrast, despite the evils of the South African apartheid regime, when it ended, Nelson Mandela chose *hope* instead of hate – a true follower of the teachings of Yeshua (Jesus).

The lack of ethnic harmony was copied from the parent country in both the eastern central African scenario, and the Russian examples in the policy of divide and rule, initially imported by the parent country. In the central African scenario, the granting of independence to the dependent territories in the process of decolonisation was not on a political majority but on *ethnic majority.* In addressing the political aspect the white minority lacked specific provisions for their protection and exclusion from integration into the mainstream society. Perhaps no other group in the newly independent countries suffered exclusion as white persons who were born and raised in those areas, back to three generations or more. In the eastern central African scenario, exclusion was carried out by means of detention of white individuals without due process of law and deportations, though they had adopted the English legal system - power and privilege corrupts the human mind, above the inherent two little gremlins that beset every human mind regardless of rank: fear and ignorance. Yet, Western European powers turned a blind eye to the predicament of the white minority.

This sad state of affairs was combined with the amendment of the British nationality laws (British Nationality Act 1948), designed to exclude certain white Britons from entering the United Kingdom; while Britain gave asylum, within the United Kingdom, to indigenous persons misplaced by the effects of granting independence to those areas. The asylum included persons who were not from the areas of British administration - the British core of fairness to "misplaced individuals (?)"

In the Russian situation, rife was "ethnic cleansing," an abhorrent phrase of inhuman cruelty. The new rulers were threatened, not by external danger but by their inner natures and desires from *ignorance* bred from unwarranted *fear* - the two little gremlins that crop up now and again. Contrast the examples of decolonisation with the Northern Ireland community, whose status was undefined and may be differentiated by the resort to violence. The dissenting minority view reflected the subjective opinion of terrorism and highlighted the degenerate situation in Northern Ireland. It was not so much as anti-Catholic or anti-Protestant but in that part of the world religion was the *difference* and became the exclusionary factor. Given the Northern Ireland situation current terrorism in Britain was not an entirely novel situation, albeit unreasonably focused on a different religion, Islam. Discrimination against the perceived or created 'other' has an established history in the British Isles. The ongoing conflict between England and Ireland generated a long-standing tradition of colonial propaganda that presented the Irish as primitive and almost animal, which stretched from medieval commentators in the twelfth century and continued through the massacre of the Irish in Ulster in the sixteenth century. Even before their formal expulsion from England in 1290.

The Irish Republican Army during the troubles in Northern Ireland may be placed in the category of 'freedom-fighters' or terrorists not unlike the Jewish Zealots such as `Simon the Zealot' or the Tamil Tigers in Sri Lanka. Ethnocentrism in Europe, beginning from the second half of the twentieth century, because of the tumultuous effects of granting independence to African countries, existed in the combination of ethnic and minority in Europe - a fact of *difference*. Since the disintegration of the Russian empire a large number of Eastern Europeans went to the West. The majority of them were white and suffered less racial discrimination than those from the former empires of non-white areas because skin colour in that scenario was not an obvious *difference*.

African Black History commenced in the era of Elizabeth 1, when she issued an open letter to the Lord Mayor of London in 1596 stating there were "too many Blackmoors in London" and ordered that they be deported from the country (according to documents in the National Archives and Gustav Ungere 2008). The Aliens Act of 1905 was to keep Britain `British' from `asylum seeking' Jews fleeing persecution from Russia and Poland. Racist riots against blacks can also be traced to 1919 in Liverpool. The shooting by the police of Jean Jimenez on the London public underground transport was fuelled by the guilt read into the somatic and characteristic traits of the victim: *difference*. Had he been blond would he have been mistaken for a terrorist and shot? Agents or servants of institutions operate by licence of the latter in dealing with the public and take the brunt of the short comings of a system. Like all other institutional entities including the personal view of the agent, the ugly consequences of a perceived *difference* rolls independently on. The racial killing of a black British man, Stephen Lawrence, from south east London while he was waiting for a bus in the evening in 1993 is one of the saddest racial incidents in Britain.

It was not till twenty years later that the perpetrators were convicted in 2012. This was possible due to profound cultural changes and to attitudes to racism, but most importantly, a change in the law of double jeopardy in 2005 in Britain, prior to which one could not be tried twice for the same crime.

In the case of the slave trading which took Africans to America, the absolute poverty of the slaves, and their underprivileged position, were assured by the very nature of the migration. It is almost impossible for adults to adapt to new linguistic and cultural skills. They would remain relatively unskilled in the language and culture of the new society they join; and it is absolutely impossible for them to get to the centre of a system of wealth, prestige, let alone hierarchy. The beginning of black immigration of the 1950s and 1960s into the UK, was the 1948 boat *Empire Windrush,* followed by the riots of 1958. The irony was that these were Commonwealth citizens invited over to help the `mother country', in manual labour, of course, after the end of World War 2. The immigrants were confronted with `No Blacks', as doors shut in their faces, wherever they went for accommodation and public places like restaurants and pubs.

An important factor in Britain is that the African Caribbean people were powerful agencies in fighting racism which began in 1959 by rights activist such as Claudia Jones, who highlighted the importance of taking a pride in identifying heritage and celebrating `blackness'. This was in resistance to the transatlantic slave trade, which lasted for well over three hundred years - from this was born the Notting Hill Carnival, which became a regular event from the mid 1960s.

But racism appears to be something that is difficult to eradicate, despite that the UDHR gained momentum by the horrors of human rights atrocities such as the Holocaust. Similar situations to the holocaust have taken place in other countries: the ethnic cleansing in Eastern Europe; the Hutu and Tutsi conflict, a blemish on the twentieth century, on the killing of 80,000 to 200,000 Hutus by the Tutsi army in Burundi in 1972 to 1994; Rwanda genocide in which Hutu militias targeted Tutsis, resulting in a 100-day death toll between 800,000 and 1 million people; Pol Pot's Khymer Rouge from 1975 to 1979 in the `killing fields' of Cambodia; and others over the decades.

BRITAIN DOES NOT hold a monopoly on racism though early British legislation to address the issue of racism was a `pussy-footing' exercise. It only partially addressed the problem of *difference*: native and immigrant, though `native' was popularly used by the uninitiated Britons to describe black immigrants in differentiating them from white non-British or non-English who they described as `foreign' - the *ignorance* of the little gremlin to equate 'black' with 'native'. The 1962 Commonwealth Immigrants Act regulated immigrants coming into the UK in terms of housing, jobs and crime problems. The first Race Relations Act 1965 was more about 'relations' rather than 'racism'. Under Labour it was made unlawful to deny access on racial grounds in public places such as hotels, restaurants, pubs, cinemas or public transport and a criminal offence for stirring up racial hatred - `incitement', but excluded racism in the workplace or housing. The Race Relations Act along with the first Race Relations Board marked a beginning in Equality and Diversity legislation in the UK under Labour.

Now a black man looks at both sides of the coin: he can go to a football match and not worry about being black. When a black player scores a goal on a British football pitch he is hailed

'British'. The racist attack on Stephen Lawrence and failure of the law enforcement agencies to bring the perpetrators to justice puts us back to the 1950s and 1960s. Reasonable people rejoiced that justice had been done, albeit at long last, when those responsible for the death of Stephen Lawrence had been brought to justice. However, spirits were dampened by media reports that there was an admission by a former deputy assistant commissioner who headed up the Metropolitan Police racial and violent crimes task force had given permission for a smear campaign against the Lawrence family. Was it not enough that the Lawrence family lost their son under such circumstances?

Most recently the verdict in the case involving a black person Trayvon Martin (26 February 2012) in the United States caused a stir as some found the outcome 'questionable' when his killer (white) was acquitted on the ground of self-defence, a case that divided public opinion. O J Simpson (black) was acquitted for the alleged murder of his ex-wife and her friend (white), a case described as the most publicised criminal trial in American history. In these two cases, it is not easy to distinguish or find a reason for racism.

We are now in the first quarter of the twenty-first century and racism still crops up here and there and in some instances based on 'assumption'. According to the *Hollywood Reporter* and other media news a Zurich shop assistant refused to show a handbag to billionaire media mogul and one of the world's richest women, Oprah Winfrey, because 'it was too expensive' for her. Perhaps it may be reasonable to assume – though assumptions make a fool out of you and I! - that because of universal redundancies by employers who expect one attendant to do jobs of those made redundant, as well as his or her own job, and be grateful that she/he was not made redundant, was a cause of `fatigue' to the shop attendant: that she had no time for anything else, hence never heard of Oprah and applied the `racial' syndrome – one of the two little gremlins, *ignorance* that beset most of us in aiding *difference*.

Likewise the controversial government poster campaign on vans around six London boroughs in July 2013 stating:

"In the UK illegally? Go home or face arrest".

One wonders if those officials responsible ever thought about the issue of `unscrupulous employers' who employ illegal immigrants and pay them a pittance because they cannot complain, they are in Britain illegally – or is it a matter of the untouchable characteristic of those at the tree top?

> *"The pursuit of riches and increase of wealth has not reduced human suffering."* Dalai Lama.

There is a time when *difference* must be recognised and emphasised: the kitchen from the bathroom. There are numerous other examples. But we all have a common enemy regardless of rank, such as natural calamities or the strike of an epidemic disease, for example ebola, though the poor suffer most in such situations. Response by international great powers, and the mega rich, had been rather slow to the ebola situation - prosaic in the bastion of privilege and wealth. Calamity is blind to any *difference:*

" *...for he maketh his sun to rise on the evil and on the good and sendeth rain on the just and on the unjust.".* Matthew 5:45

There is also a proverb in ChiChewa (a language of eastern central Africa):

"Dzidze pano nza tonse = what may come befalls us all."

When abroad a few Britons found the *difference* between themselves, and the so-called natives so great that they went beyond snobbery and engaged in barbaric acts which the mother country as a regime did not practise. Even today where individuals exceed in the *Peregrini syndrome* Lady Britannia finds it intolerable.

IN INDIA in the Amritsar massacre of 379 innocent Indians (1919) when Winston Churchill referred to the incident as `monstrous'; the British government condemned it; Indo-British relations permanently scarred; and it was the prelude to Gandhi's non-cooperation movement (1920-22). During his visit to the Sikh Golden Temple at Amritsar in 2013, Premier Cameron 'almost' apologised for Britain's imperial past. Contrast with Malawi Martyrs Day 3rd March 1959, established to commemorate forty (population 4 million in 1958) people who were shot in 1959 during the uprising against British colonialism, particularly the Federation of Rhodesia and Nyasaland, a political amalgamation of Nyasaland (Malawi), Southern Rhodesia (Zimbabwe) and Northern Rhodesia (Zambia).

The shooting was carried out by four `trigger happy' young white Rhodesian soldiers who where deployed by the British government to quell the uprising (during the British Empire days, troops could be deployed from a nearby area).

Posterity cannot be responsible for the mistakes of its ancestors. To apologise for the past mistakes of British administration abroad is a useless exercise, condescending and paternalistic. Those incidents spell the characteristic of imperialism, a Roman legacy - a fact of *difference* between the ruler and the ruled. Should Britain, or any regime for that matter, apologise for the mistakes of its ancestors to all those other countries for atrocities committed by individual agents?

When Britain or America invades other countries in the twenty-first century, without a United Nations mandate or consultation with Parliament, in the example of Blair/Bush invasion of Iraq, then the question `why' should be asked.

WITH THE PASSAGE OF TIME the current view evolved and it became widely accepted that differences between cultures were differences between races (or peoples, used synonymously). European nineteenth century observers, with all the might of advanced industrial civilisation behind them, when they came into contact with non-industrialised peoples in the world (the Australian Aborigines as the yardstick for frequent citation) the *difference* seemed so great. From the fifties to early sixties onwards, predominantly among Western European intellectuals, the notion of racism evolved to the view that differences between peoples were the product of cultural or social conditioning, rather than a biological aspect.

It had been held for a long time that the Neanderthals were not as intelligent as modern man but this view has changed, and it is now conjectured that they may have been more intelligent than modern man. The debate between archaeologist, anthropologists and humanists will continue as new evidence is uncovered.

Racism has now evolved to the state where it is seen as unfashionable and anti-racism is regarded by many as a virtue. They seek `racist' statements everywhere and this leads in turn to a form of `internal racism', which is as prejudicial as being racist. It has the same features - gang mentality and influenced by received external opinion. But an important question is how is it going now that we have arrived at the fiftieth anniversary of Martin Luther King's Address:

"I Have A Dream," at the March on Washington, D C on 28 August 1963 for God's children: black, white, Jews, Gentiles, Protestants and Catholics..?

Perhaps the answer to the Dream is that the situation has evolved from slavery to a non white man in the White House; but the gap between the privileged and the rest has grown and continues to grow – *mammon worship* at the tree top, which has become the ruler, as opposed to the rest and it is the disease of the twenty-first century.

European empires took the reigns of power, ended contemporary atrocities in those areas, and introduced a modern Western civilisation. In the late 1950s, with new African leaders of the newly independent state compromised, and by the cudgel of ethnicity, black leaders penalised Europeans and other non-blacks, despite their presence for several generations in the new states. For almost a century of European rule of Africa a wonderful opportunity to build an equal multi-racial cultural society was lost. But then in that particular era, the *difference* between ruler and ruled, was so great that such a notion was unthinkable. Instead colonialism outlived itself by the inevitable evolution of human understanding.

Had the colonists, right from the outset, educated the indigenous people, perhaps colonisation would not have outlived itself, instead with educated locals, all would have lived in harmony; but in hindsight we can all be clever.

IN HIS SPEECH AT THE LABOUR CONFERENCE on 27 September 2005 Premier Blair echoed the *Dual Mandate* trade exchange for Africa, independently from that put forward by Dr

Livingstone and Frederick Lugard, one hundred and fifty-four years ago. Unfortunately, most of the media were more taken up by the almost outline draft of a Blair biography. Yet again, the proposal fell on deaf ears.

The proposal that legitimate trade would replace the slave trade was the precept of application for both the East Coast and Atlantic trade. There were mixed views to this proposal. That it was a camouflage for European economic self-interest had been disputed. Dr David Livingstone believed in the exchange of British manufactured goods for legitimate products of Africa as the best way by which the "Africans would attain civilisation". Likewise, Frederick Lugard's *Dual Mandate*, indicating that the interests of Europeans and Africans were essentially complementary, had fallen on deaf ears. Some European agents of government on the spot, by failure to give credence to anything indigenous, undermined the fairness of Western European rule in Africa, like some individuals to the present day - the front line violators of human rights.

A fitting example is, Queen Victoria's representative, the governor of the Gold Coast, modern Ghana, demanded that he should sit on the sacred Golden Stool. This led to war and he was replaced. He took no trouble to understand the significance of the Golden Stool, that it had never been a throne but a shrine and symbol of the Spirit of the Ashanti people of the Gold Coast. Julia Maitland writing from Madras, India, between 1836 and 1839 said of Indians:

"Their civility is disagreeable but the rudeness and contempt with which the English

treat them are quite painful to witness."

North American immigrants derided the indigenous people, the

Indians; Australians treated the aborigines less than human; and throughout Africa manual labour was equated with the black race.

Since the early 1960s it became fashionable to deride Britain and other Western European powers for colonisation. There is nothing wholly good or wholly bad, but a matter of balancing, – in 'good' or 'bad' there is a big *difference*. The motivation was vision at a time when in their narrow world they envisaged that until white men from Europe, as Christians, had stepped upon a piece of land, it remained for all reasonable purposes, undiscovered, heathen and condemned.

Many ancient atrocities were removed by colonisation. The presence of Britain, more so than that of her contemporary empires, brought relief and peace in certain aspects including things affecting women. In India, the practice of placing a live widow on her husband's funeral pyre ceased. The international slave trade still existed in the mid-1800s on the east coast of Africa, despite that Britain had abolished slavery in 1807 by an Act of Parliament, led by Wilberforce. By the efforts of Dr Livingstone, international slave trade on the east coast of Africa ended. Nineteenth-century Europeans regarded these atrocities as shocking, "what would have been, to some, part of the fabric of life to their own recent ancestors". Perhaps *Cifwamba*, kidnap, was one of the greatest terrors of Africa. Individuals separated from their clans and enslaved to enhance the following of a distant king's or chief's clan, long before international slavery was envisaged; victims to witchcraft; human sacrifice rituals; and *mwabvi*, the witch-hunt poison; in eastern central Africa, beautiful healthy maidens chosen to be buried alive with and for the dead chief's personal comforts in the underworld.

"The women of eastern central Africa lived in constant fear of

being stolen", so said Livingstone, though in the above scenario they were not stolen, but were members of the chief's clan. Colonisation put an end to these customs but compare, in Europe, mutilation punishment was referred to as 'hanged, quartered and drawn', a form of atrocity.

Legal Bodies

Legal bodies are no less biased to age, race and gender and apply the *difference* diplomatically which is equivalent to `hypocrisy'. As a follow up on her request in a legal magazine for comments on ageism, the editor of the magazine put out an independent and personal article concerning pupillage. The response was tremendous. She asked as to whether the Bar reflected that by 2011 most people in the UK would be over 40 and the possibility that the state pension could be raised to 70; and that there was age discrimination at the Bar for as young as 30 and in some instances even younger. Most legal bodies including commercial organisations use a form that asks an applicant to indicate their cultural background before returning the form - a form used by organisations in the private and public sectors. Given the appallingly low numbers of ethnic minorities and women who have aspired to the professions they have studied for, let alone the apex category, one wonders what is the real reason and purpose for requesting applicants' cultural background on application forms? The forms ask for applicant's age immediately after the space for name. One may expect that the requirement for age would be more appropriate for Scotland Yard in the detection of crime or for the hospitals in the administration of medicine. Section two of the form begins with school education. Once an applicant has qualified as a barrister the relevancy of primary school attended is unclear, save as an *inclusion device* which in effect is *exclusion*, the `cosy club' syndrome. Some HR departments have changed this practice.

Given the dynamics of population growth in all its multi-aspects the older people can contribute to the economy, if they so wished as tax-payers rather than seen as a burden upon the tax-payer; and as useful participants who could bring experience and stability to the workforce to the benefit of the community as a whole.

In Britain related increase in crime and civil wrongs, apparently reflects plenty of room at the practice arena - or in other than the crime and civil wrongs scenario, at the work place in the commercial field. It had become the practice in handing out current employment questionnaires, and in other surveys, in most organisations to include the question on `sexual orientation': an intrusive and adolescent question. Why does `sexual orientation' have to be everybody's business? Most probably for similar reasons: eligibility for `inclusion', to exclude homosexuals?

A male chairman and a female secretary of a legal organisation were found guilty of race and gender bias against a female Asian permanent employee. Other abounding examples include the Fire Brigade, homophobia, the lack of promotion of women to managerial positions. Even in the BBC, women presenters must be off the air or screen when they reach age fifty, while the men are venerated. Universally, nations have long become detached from the rudimentary system of economy, barter, in the exchange of commodities prior to the lucre as the nexus. Every vocation fills a vacuum in providing a service essential to some individual. It does not matter whether it is an occupation or a profession the ultimate goal is the market place.

Ageism

On ageism women and men are almost equally discriminated

against, as with gender, race and minority. Evidence suggests that aging is a genetic factor, and not all people age at the same rate; nor do all wish to retire at the government set statutory age of retirement.

Ageism is socially conditioned, coupled with a particular attitude in the resignation to a socially structured dependency; and fettered by the slots into which the aged are categorised, highlighting a *difference* under ageism in institutions. This disregards the merits of a combination of qualifications and experience, and is a form of stereotyping. Ageism in its assumptions is seen as a social problem and beset with fear of what life presents naturally. Language may be politically correct in paying lip service to a culture of equal opportunities. The reality is that it is not easy to find organisations or employment institutions which do not directly or indirectly discriminate against ageism. By age requirement on employment application forms, the candidate fails to attain the vital initial stage, that of an interview where one could prove oneself in person.

Given the dynamics of population growth in all its multi-aspects, the aged could contribute to the economy, if they so wished as tax-payers rather than seen as a burden upon the tax-payer; and as useful participants who could bring experience and stability to the workforce to the benefit of the community as a whole.

Such shortcomings are also apparent in insurance policies for travel, vehicle, and others. The `exclusion' list is long. The situation has changed since the passage of age retirement legislation and the elderly are employed to work where many have been made redundant. One of the reasons they are able to obtain employment is that they can be paid less than a younger employee – self interest at the top of the tree.

The rise in life expectancy, the falling birth rates and the growth of the aging population in Britain and other countries had led to a significant increase in academic and professional awareness in the study of aging. Theoretical attempts had been made to redefine what old age meant and to seek new attitudes about older people in providing health and social services.

The over sixty and the under sixteen outnumber the rest of the population in Britain. By 2011 most people were over forty and by 2025 pensioners are expected to outnumber children by nearly two million (Cunningham). Britain, like other Western industrialised countries, had suffered from the division of an aging population and a deficit workforce, but this is now history, because employers have turned to making people redundant – reduction of the workforce by design. To assess people by the number of years they have lived without giving them the opportunity of an interview on the evidence of written biographic information alone, regardless of their merits, experience and excellence on professional or occupational performance, may be construed as *benign apartheid* based on a *difference*.

AS LONG AS THE SUN RISES and sets each day, those endowed with long life will surely arrive at the *obsolete object* milestone. This phrase may appear to be unkind but there are those who treat the aged as such. At that stage one becomes a different person, and there is a *difference* in physical appearance, and in almost every aspect. We only have to look at some figures historically to find the meaning of 'obsolete object'.

In her old age, Queen Victoria's life was beset with much sadness: the untimely death of her forty-seven year old husband at the prime of his life. Underneath all the pomp and pageantry there was a 'human being', a fact to which all around her were oblivious, like she was some obsolete object. John Brown her Scottish personal servant was appreciated by many, including the Queen, for his competence and companionship but he was also resented by many for his influence and informal manner, without a thought as to the solace he gave to the Queen.

The exact relationship between Victoria and Brown was the subject of much speculation by contemporaries and continues to be controversial today, albeit to a lesser degree because of the passage of time. The 1997 film *Mrs. Brown*, a fictionalised story of John Brown, played by Billy Connolly, and Judi Dench, as Victoria, well portrays this.

After the death of Brown Victoria found solace in Abdul Karim whom she regarded as a son. He was the son of a hospital assistant and was one of two Indian men selected to become servants to the Queen in 1887, her Golden Jubilee year. Like Brown, Karim became Victoria's favourite and she called him `Munshi' (`clerk' or `teacher' in Urdu) and later appointed him her secretary within the Royal Household. Servants generally, but particularly those in Victorian households, suffered from a `household ownership' syndrome in an exclusive clan, wielding a power within their domain. A situation exported to the colonies, where servants were the locals. It should be noted that a servant is a 'friend', whether in commoner or royal household, who knows everything about the employer.

In their collective imagination the members of the household were superior to Abdul, a 'foreigner', not only a cultural but also a racial *difference*. The Queen wanted to give Abdul a knighthood but it was out of the question - unthinkable. Today knighthoods and other accolades are dished out to the least imaginable – but everything has its time. The British colonial `upper class' context mimicked the Victorian era culture in their households, contrast: the `Dona' (`lady' in Portuguese or Spanish, adopted by African countries exposed to Portuguese influence, the label for all non-black women: to the local non-black, but non-white dona 'a' was added 'aDona' to distinguish her from the European dona) of the house offers a cup of tea to a non-white person. In the typical British, or English, if you like, politeness, she apologises:

"I am so sorry he [the servant] has brought you one without a handle." She pours out the tea from a pot, then she says:

"You can go and have it in the pantry", extending the filled handle-less cup and saucer. The pantry was one up from the kitchen, the latter the place for the servants - hierarchy to a fine art! This Dona got the wrong end of the upper class stick, as one may reasonably say, she was in the minority. It would, therefore, be unfair to say the majority were like her. In fact, the majority were dignified and reasonable, and some, made good friends with the locals, friendships that lasted long after they left the colonised areas.

For Margaret Thatcher in her old age, the `obsolete object' aspect emerged: she was a different person in a different world, like all those who age. *The Iron Lady,* starring Meryl Streep, was a film that made much of her dementia in old age, while her achievements as Prime Minister were bypassed. Albeit her achievements entrenched the "Us" and "Them" syndrome that enriched the rich and impoverished the rest. While the power of the trade unions was broken, and now employees have no protection – the Thatcherite legacy. Nonetheless, the movie failed to highlight her qualities as a premier.

6 - MINORITIES

There are a good number of minority groups within Britain and around the world who suffer discrimination in different ways and in varying degrees according to their particular circumstances and the nature of the societies and the areas where they live. It is a historical fact that over the centuries there has always been some group or groups of people that have and are shunned or persecuted because of a *difference* between them and mainstream society.

Travellers: Roma and Gypsy

The majority of people appear to be unaware that people known as Travellers or Gypsies are comprised of two totally different groups of people who share one thing in common a `nomadic' existence or "Travellers" as they are called. There is a *difference* between them and mainstream society in that they pursue their own values distinct from those of the mainstream society. The two groups are Roma, nothing to do with Romans, and Gypsy, the latter are of Irish origin. The Roma people originated from northern India and speak Romany, a Sanskrit language. They are of Jewish heritage, and many are now going back to Israel, to make "ALLEJAH", Prophesy of the Diaspora returning to Israel, the Promised Land. In tandem with the rest of the growth of world population, these two small groups of "Travellers" have substantially increased. They are also found mostly in Europe, North Africa, North America and other places. The English titled them `Gypsy' from the word `Egypt' or `Egyptian', mistakenly thinking they came from Egypt, because of their dark skin colour and nomadic lifestyle. The French, Italian and Spanish labelled them Tsigani or Citano in describing and naming the `Gypsy'; while in India the Roma are called the Dalit.

The India's caste system is not unlike the classes of Britain. There are seven social castings of people in India: the highest being the Brahmans: Maharajah = `jah' equivalent to God in Hebrew and the lowest being the untouchables but the Dalit were regarded as even lower than the untouchables. All castes as classes present a *difference,* and by those who regard them as different exercise a form of *apartheid:* a word that simply means *"exclusion"* which the South African Boer government grasped as the policy of racial segregation. There are around 300,000 Roma and Gypsy Travellers in the UK. Since 2002, Travellers have been legally recognised as an ethnic group and are protected under the *Race Relations Act.* England has mapped and listed every Traveller caravan site in and around England. There are more caravan sites in the east of England according to latest statistics. Those who belong to the Travellers community believe that there are more travellers than the statistics show.

The report published by the Department for Communities and Local Government, is the most comprehensive count of local Travellers and includes both those on authorised and unauthorised sites. A total of 15,274 are recorded and those on authorised sites increased by 556 caravans since January 2010. Unauthorised sites hugely dropped to 26% on the previous year and a much smaller decline of 8% on land owned by either Roma or Gypsy Travellers.

The Roma speak Romanes which has nothing to do with Romans or Italy. Romanes is spoken by every true Roma world-wide and they are four major dialects from four different tribes: Sinti, Kalderash, Romungro and Lovari. In Britain the Romany language has been infused with English, Gaelic and Welsh languages. Both the Roma and Gypsy are a marginalised and little-understood segment of society. *Ignorance* and *fear*, those two little gremlins, regardless of rank. Plus the lack of integration with the main stream society, has caused great problems for both sides: Travellers and main stream society.

For the *difference* between the mainstream society and minorities, the latter's suffering has not been so benign, especially when they have been evicted from areas where they have briefly settled. They had been blamed, based upon assumptions, for thefts that may take place near the areas where they have settled.

Problems such as being discriminated against, poor health and poverty are faced by Travellers who are viewed with hatred and suspicion, as some call them 'vermin'. Roma people were to be shot on sight, and also they were enslaved, hence they have Welsh and English names and surnames, and like the descendants of African slaves, they had their own Romany names before enslavement.

Roma or Gypsy have been great world Evangelists, as they spread the Gospel naturally on their travels, and they are still doing that today. The Roma or Gypsy people were killed in the Holocaust equally with the Jews, but unlike the Jews, hardly mentioned, or made public, because of their derided status: a situation similar to that of black people whose fate or noble deeds were not worthy of mention.

At twilight on 2 August 1944 at Auschwitz-Birkenau Gipsy camp, Nazis liquidated the camp killing 3,000 Roma and Sinti, in the gas chambers. The prisoners were given a sausage and a piece of bread and told they were being taken to another camp but they doubled back towards the killing factories.

THE YEAR 2006 MARKED the 350th anniversary of the readmission of Jewish people to England in 1656 by Oliver Cromwell. By the edict of King Edward 1, they had been banished altogether from England in 1290, prior to which they had been subjected to periods of severe persecution and discrimination. Under Church law the Jews were required to wear a patch of white cloth to distinguish them from Christians. One cannot help wondering, whether these church leaders ever understood the meaning of the pacific words of Yeshua, whom they called Jesus Christ?

Jews have been living in England since Roman and Anglo-Saxon times, but became an organised community after William the Conqueror's arrival in 1066 when the King had encouraged Jewish merchants and artisans to move from northern France to England. In the England of the 1950s, while doors in London were being shut in the faces of the West Indians, doors were opened to students from the Western European colonies. The Jewish community in England received foreign students like they were members of their family, and included them in social events. Particularly in what was then known as the "Jews' Paradise" in Golders Green: the landlady, a kindly 'Jewish Mama', gave one an insight into the life and times of the Jews.

Since the times of King William 1 the Jews had made such a great impact in the economic contribution to the country over the years by their expertise, which led the Jews to say of Britain:

"It is their king, but our country."

Conscientious Objectors

Conscientious objectors are of the many minority groups who are obedient to conscience on a number of grounds: freedom of thought, conscience, and/or religion as they refuse to participate in a combatant capacity in any war. Conscientious objectors have been derided and seen as cowards and in earlier times had been executed for refusing to participate in a combatant capacity. Though now they may be required to perform an alternative service to the country in a civilian or non-combatant capacity. There is a *difference* between conscientious objectors and those who bow to the inevitability of wars dreamed up by leaders – but in the defence of one's country is another matter.

A judge's statement in an Edinburgh court sums up the former attitude towards two conscientious objectors while sentencing them to one year imprisonment:

"...the dastardliness and cowardice of the offence..."

The two men in the dock were James Maxton who was arrested for supporting strikes at arms factories along with James McDougal.   In 1966 Muhammad Ali commenting on the American unpopular Viet Nam war, gave his own definition:

"I ain't got no quarrel with them Viet Cong ... They never called me Nigger."

The United Nations Commission on Human Rights officially broadened the international definition of conscientious objection, which was officially clarified in 1995.

Siegfried Sassoon, a war hero, threw his military cross into the Mersey and refused further military duties but as a well-connected person, he was declared mentally ill. A private soldier in a similar situation, would have been court marshalled and shot – Father Time brought us to this milestone. Sassoon's poems paint a vivid picture of the horror of war as poems of his friend Robert Graves in his revelation that British soldiers savagely murdered German prisoners of war.

It was a breath of fresh air to read of Alex Salmond's 'olive branch' policy when, as leader for Scotland's National Party

(SNP), said that an independent Scotland government by SNP would promote peace rather than war; that the constitution would outlaw nuclear weapons and would require democratic approval for military action – sadly he did not make it to the executive desk.

Smokers and non-smokers

Smokers created a *difference* since the banning of smoking in public and most areas. Some, approving the smoking ban, put down to `gullible' consumers as who puff away their earnings. Would it not be better to put a stop to cigarette manufacturing than to penalise individual smokers? No, it is very lucrative for the producers at every stage of cigarette production, and for the revenue it brings but not for the labourers in the plantation of tobacco. Tobacco is the Noxious Weed – extract from author's poem on the Noxious Weed:

"...out into the cold...the noxious weed to puff...

Harvesters...manufacturers...reaped their profit,

...polity collected her revenue..."

(see *Little Book of Poetry*)

Seller and Buyer

In seller and Buyer lies a *difference*. Some sellers have become indifferent to but yet focused on a *difference* between themselves and `buyers'. The very category that got them or would get them to the top of the tree. They make employees in their organisations redundant without realising, or should one say caring, that by such action they are neglecting the buyer. Some take the *"I'm alright Jack'* attitude that has become the novel culture in our contemporary society, joining the rank of some bankers and some members of the Westminster Parliament.

If ten years ago one had predicted that corruption would creep into the Westminster Parliament, the mother of democracy and of Parliaments, `bonkers' would have come to one's mind. Likewise, if one had said the same of the bankers. The latter, in the face of adversity, were treated like special people who were irreplaceable.

No one is indispensable, and this lies in the statement:

"The King is dead. Long live the King! (or Queen)"

Nonetheless, it is well to remember that Westminster and the majority of banks, as institutions, are not barrels of apples where a few bad ones would contaminate the lot, but most see them as tinted.

In recent times it has become fashionable for some sellers regardless of their size to sell perishables that are well past sell by date. Between the seller and buyer, or consumer, there is a *difference* which motivates the seller to hold the consumer to ransom whereby the latter is obliged by necessity, particularly on fresh food, to pay what the seller demands.

They create a fictitious `scarcity' scenario in commodities, the lever to entice buyers. They are more concerned about `profit' and forget that without a buyer there could be no sale, and no sale, no profit, and place themselves above the buyer who seeks to buy their goods.

Goods can be defined as a `good' that one can have in a variety of things.  Goods are things people want and classified in two groups: `tangible', necessities such as food and clothing which are created through value addition and can be bought or sold at a price; or luxuries which one can do without, aside from services which are `intangible'.

People have many wants but most lack or have limited resources with which to acquire wants and desires. The *difference* between desires and resources creates *scarcity* and the world does not hold an infinite amount of resources. If people want more of a good than there is available a problem arises. A `good' is a product that contains the expenditure of `opportunity cost' in it's production, such as utilities, wages, transport and other. By placing themselves on this side of the *difference* between seller and buyer the seller throws away residual food than to lower the price; or places them on a table market "To Clear" - but proof of the freshness of the item is in the eating.

Constantly perishables are well past sale by date – although they carry no such label. The market is flooded with, as never before seen, merchandise - quantity void of quality.

BOYCOTT, AN ENGLISH AND FORMER British soldier, gave his name to the household word. He was an estate agent of the Earl of Erne in County Mayo, Ireland, an absentee landowner of a group of landowners who held most of the land in Ireland. Boycott was chosen by Charles Parnell, an Irish politician in the fall of 1880 to be the test case for a new policy on land reform.

Any landlord who refused to charge lower rents or any tenant who took over the farm of an evicted tenant would be shunned by Parnell's supporters. By Boycott's strong sense of duty to his employer, he stuck to higher rents and evicted tenants who could not pay. Parnell's Irish Land League stepped in and 'isolated' Boycott and his family, without servants, farmhands, mail delivery and other services. 'Boycott' entered the English dictionary extending to other languages: French, Dutch, German, and Russian.

Employer and Employee

Employees are not exactly in the minority, in fact, they are in the majority to employers based on numbers; but they are a minority in comparison to the power of employers. Cabinet and Parliament and top jobs both in government and the private sector, are headed by a greater number of white male middle class Oxbridge members. The media headline statistics speak for themselves: for *political correctness,* only a smattering of ethnic minorities are in top jobs, a category to which women including non-white are relegated. Countries of former empires also mimicked this style in reverse, against the whites, especially soon after independence from Western European powers.

We are beholden to our institutions in all we do in our daily existence: be it banking, shopping, utilities, broadband, telephone and TV in our homes, without which we could not survive in a modern society. The *difference* between supplier and consumer – though the latter *pays* for the service.

Since the beginning of civilisation the so-called public servants around the world live on standards much higher than those of the public they serve: expensive servants. This is why it becomes difficult to achieve accountability in the established *status quo* of institutions.

This system of administration also applies to trading institutions in the private sector, where the gap between the `board' and the `shop floor' is massive – without the shop floor the board could not survive and vice versa.

Under the law (1799 and 1800) all trade union activity was illegal and subject to three months imprisonment by the justices of the peace. When David Lloyd George took office (1916) as Liberal prime minister mergers and amalgamations were made, leading to the creation of new legislation. Prior to this, the power of the trade unions was unthinkable, the *difference* between employer and employee was so great then.

Margaret Thatcher's emergence as Britain's first female premier – the Iron Lady - sent shocks not only in Britain but across the world. The cabinet papers had recently been released under the 30-year rule (*The Guardian* 01/08/13) and other media reports. They indicate how she took a grip on her ministers, and the country, in her belligerent style and hostility, particularly on the power of the trade unions, headed by Arthur Scargill. Her instructions to her ministers: "lose no opportunity in eroding trade union membership." As a result of the Thatcher policy employees have largely been without protection.

Though at least, each on the top shelf of her and his career, Thatcher and Scargill had one thing in common, the silver Mark X Jaguar in which she was chauffeur driven. He drove his – redundancies and the rich getting richer is the 'Thatcher legacy'.

The landmark ruling by the Employment Appeal Tribunal that overtime should be included in holiday pay centred on the case of *Bear Scotland v Fulton*; where employees claimed that their voluntary overtime should have been included in their holiday pay. This decision effectively changes the law so that organisations would now include regular non-guaranteed overtime payments when calculating holiday pay. Prior to this, only a worker's basic pay counted towards calculation.

The prevailing *difference* between employer and employee is that the former is in a position to make redundancies and expect fewer employees to do the work of several people. Each day has only twenty-four hours and no one individual has the physical and mental strength to do all that is expected of them – perhaps Hercules...

The strength of seller or employer may appear to be greater than buyer or employee but neither side can survive without the other. It does not matter where you go in the shops, there may be four check-out points but only one attendant – three have been made redundant. Your heart bleeds for the one in attendance: the expression in her (or his) eyes spell `exhaustion', while they try to do their best with a smile - modern slavery.

The telephone is programmed to replace the telephonist giving the caller several options, except one on 'complaints' – no personal touch – the age of technology...The *difference* between seller and buyer is apparent where consumers are constantly frustrated by waiting to be served at a counter without an attendant and more often than not they give up and walk away. One wonders how much sales the seller loses in this sort of scenario – perhaps they are rich enough and could not care less.

Henry Stewart, a leading publisher of vocational journals that support employ-ability and career development, argues that bad management blights the working lives of millions of people, and that the solution is to let everyone choose their own bosses. Wishful thinking, democracy is not a concept that is extended to the *difference* between employer and employee; or seller and buyer. The consequence of a free market. Redundancy is not only down to replacement of manpower by the introduction of new technology whereby the post can be handled by a machine; the slowing down of business on production or sales; relocation of business; some changes take place such as a merger for example; reorganisation or a host of other reasons. We live on a planet of 'relativity' and what affects the bottom is also bound to affect the top in time.

On the aspect of `authority' and `public' the councils around England have made huge profits out of a section of the public: `motorists', on increased parking charges and fines (BBC Radio 4, 31/07-03/08/13). The net parking income increases to £635 million in 2013/14. In some instances there was no mandate to make such charges. The figures were revealed after a judge had declared one London council acted illegally by using parking charges to raise revenue.

Community Secretary Eric Pickles commenting:

"Parking is not a tax or cash cow" when he pledged to take action against high parking charges in towns and cities.

But here is an all-time quote:

> *"Every man must decide whether he will walk in the light of creative altruism or in the darkness of destructive selfishness"* — Martin Luther King Jr.

Ruler and the ruled

Beautiful Marie Antoinette, wife of King Louis xvi of France, (1791-1792) in all her compassion when the people of France were starving said:

"Why not give them cake?"

Living in all the pomp and pageantry of the French court Marie Antoinette never knew the difference between `cake and bread'.

She was beheaded along with her husband when he was deposed during the French Revolution. No reasonable person would condone the `killing' of either prince or pauper, both are equal as children of God, in `humanity', the *difference* is made by man's sophistry and snobbery.

When Emperor Haile Selassie was deposed he was shown a British television documentary *The Hidden Famine* depicting thousands of the people he ruled, Ethiopians starving in Wollo, Ethiopia. The film was spliced with snippets of the Emperor and his entourage drinking champagne, eating caviar and feeding meat to his dogs from a silver platter – the Emperor went into a `pensive' mood which lasted through the rest of his life.

The Watergate political scandal of the United States of America resulted in the indictment, trial and incarceration of forty-three people, including dozens of Nixon's top administration officials. But Nixon was never apprehended in anyway – like most leaders, he went Scot free though he resigned. This is a typical example that the world is governed by a two tier system indicating a *difference*: one for the privileged and the other for the rest, regardless of country or system of government. Since then Watergate has been adopted by current journalists in attaching 'gate' to novel scandals.

Physically Challenged

In the eighteenth century an unkind view of disability prevailed. One could be transformed from `beautiful' to `deformed' overnight. Lady Mary Wortley Montague, a writer and a society beauty, caught smallpox when she was twenty-six:

"...where is the bloom that promised happiness for years to come?"

She cried. Beauty then was a moral value. Beauty is a matter of definition in the eyes of the beholder. There is no such a thing as `ugliness', only the human who harms others is ugly.

In all the above examples the fact of *difference* lies in two opposing situations where at the bottom of the tree is the vehicle by which the other attains the top of the tree. `Top of the tree' scenario applies to many situations such as the attainment of a successful position, and invariably, the pattern or the `hidden' truth is the same: affluence, opulence, comfort or the mere fame of it.

Homosexuality

The practise of homosexuality is nothing new and has been present in all societies for thousands of years. The first known recorded evidence dates back to 9660 to 5000 BC in Mesolithic rock art in Sicily showing phallic male figures in pairs. They have been interpreted variously; as hunters, acrobats, religious initiates, but all are depictions of homosexuality. Since then there is time line overwhelming evidence of lesbian, gay, bisexual and trans-gender in many cultures to the present. Homosexuality is a correlative mode of sexuality provided it is between consenting adults where there is no abuse of children. It is rather sad to see great figures of the Churches eloquently splitting over gay rights; though they do not condemn with similar vigour the priests who have sexually abused children, particularly boys.

A small percentage find members of their own gender sexually attractive. The majority of males say from boyhood onwards they felt a strong attraction to other males and never felt drawn to females (Desmond Morris).

Hence they are set apart from young boys who often play

homosexual games with their male friends but pass on to a new phase when their interest switches to girls. Confirmed homosexuals remain at the `young boys play stage'. For the first few years toddlers of both genders know no difference between male and female friends till they are four or five. Then the little boy avoids little girls who were his pals and plays only with other boys and becomes part of a boys' group. It is also possible that homosexuality tendencies may stem from the dominance of chromosomes in the zygote. In gays there may be a residual female sexuality, despite their masculine traits.

Lesbians may have determined feminine traits but there was a residual development of male traits. Lesbian presents a less complex scenario and regarded as less aggressive than gay (Morris). Homosexuals were falsely blamed for the emergence of AIDS (Acquired Immune Deficiency Syndrome) pandemic. One leader in the World Health Organisation in the early 1980s, came close to a possible theory for the emergence of the pandemic that claimed so may young lives. That it was a highly genetically variable virus which reproduced more rapidly than most other entities which translate into mutations in its genetic code; and that mutation in DNA was the cause of the emergence of AIDS. Recently, it has been said that AIDS pandemic has been traced to the 1920s in Kinshasa, modern Democratic Republic of the Congo, according to scientists; and that population growth, sex and railways allowed HIV to spread.

Some who claim to be Christian are `judges of morality' and exhibit the draconian Old Testament attitude towards homosexuality. They fail to convey the *difference* between Yeshua's (Jesus') teachings and the Roman legacy known as Jesus Christ in `Christianity'. It would be best to set aside the Old Testament and look to the New Testament; for this is the era of Yeshua and forgiveness, quoted in Matthew 7:1, 2:

"Judge not, that you be not judged."
"For with what judgment you judge, you will be judged, and with the measure you use, it will be measured back to you."

The Cleveland Street Scandal of 1889 was about a homosexual male brothel in Fitzrovia, London, discovered by police. The government was accused of covering up the scandal to protect the names of elitist and higher up patrons, including a prince. The scandal gave rise to the unreasonable attitude that male homosexuality was an aristocratic vice that corrupted lower class young men. However, this does not apply to all homosexuals. Some white men in the colonies pampered non-white youths, by giving them presents and treating them like 'young ladies'. Eighteenth-nineteenth century literature, particularly Victorian, tells in subtle language that some of the celebrities - though the word `celebrity' was not rife then - both men and women had gay and lesbian, including bisexual, affairs. Illegality in homosexuality was the blackmailer's charter and this may have influenced, to some extent, change of law in removing illegality in homosexuality in Britain. This was the death knell of the blackmailer's charter.

In some instances, both gay and lesbian, there is the tendency to dress for the appropriate schema. Some gay men like to dress as women but this in public is socially unacceptable, unlike the position of women who may freely dress as men. Most transsexuals love to adorn themselves in feminine attire and there are more male than female transsexuals.

Sappho, a Greek poet born on the island of Lesbos (630-612, died around 579 BC) famous for her lesbian themes, gave her name and homeland the definition of lesbianism. The Alexandrians included her in the list of nine lyric poets. Same gender liaisons were no different since then to now and are of the same characteristic: for and against as all societies differ in their views. The *difference* is that the twenty-first century is an era of transparency.

Plato published *Symposium* (385 BC) in which Phaedrus, Eryixmachus, Aristophanes and other Greek intellectuals debated that love between males is the highest form, while sex with women was lustful and utilitarian. Socrates differs by exercising self-control when seduced by the beautiful Alcibiades.

Alexander the Great (326 BC) conquered most of the then Western world, established the Hellenistic Age whereby many were converted to a Hellenistic culture that regarded homosexual relationships positively and as the norm in ancient Greek culture. In 498 CE, despite laws on gay sex as an offence, Christian emperors continued to collect taxes on male prostitutes up to the reign of Anastasius 1, when he finally abolished the tax in favour of best men by sampling. Thomas Aquinas (1265) regarded sodomy as second only to murder in defining sins.

Perhaps the case of Alan Turing (1912-1954), the Enigma Code breaker of the Second World War, and father of modern computer science, is among the saddest of the gays. In 1952 he was convicted of 'gross indecency' – the catch-all legal device used to prosecute any consenting sexual acts between two men. The judge gave him a choice, what seemed to be a lenient sentence at the time: a two-year prison sentence or undergo an experimental chemical castration, to remove homosexual tendencies – man's law playing God. He chose the latter so he could not be parted from his work and machine. Two years later he committed suicide. He was granted a posthumous Royal pardon by the Queen in December 2013. The relatives of Alan Turin presented a petition to Number 10 Downing Street in 2015 calling for pardons for men convicted under historical laws. Thousands of gay and bisexual men found guilty of decades-old sexual offences in England and Wales have been postmostly pardoned. Statutory pardons will also be granted to people still living who apply to have their convictions removed. (BBC Breaking News 11/02/17).

In the UK, the modern history of reforms on the laws of homosexuality has developed gradually to what it is today though it took the efforts of many to bring change. The Homosexual Law Reform Society campaigned for changes in discriminatory laws that criminalised homosexuality. The Conservative government set up a Departmental Committee in 1954 to look into aspects of British sex laws, resulting in the Wolfenden Report published in 1957. In 1958, the academic Dyson, wrote a letter to The Times calling for reform of the law by implementing the Wolfenden Committee's recommendations. This was signed by many distinguished people, plus rulings by the European Court of Justice which was repealed in full by the Equality Act 2010, which also applied to transsexuals.

The above changes were long after the trials of Oscar Wilde, who was arrested and imprisoned for gross indecency. Had Wilde not been born a hundred years or so earlier he may have escaped the penal law and the accusing finger of society. Unless his play fellows had not been consenting adults or were minors, or if he had lived in Greece, before change of the law. But society is a giant chameleon complemented by the law and its changes.

Gay men make good lasting platonic friends for women to share intellectual dialogue or a game of sport sometimes lacking in hetero-sexual men. In the gays there is no hidden agenda that may threaten the `platonic' characteristic of the friendship – pinching woman's bottom, for example. The persecution of homosexuals, like everything else, has come to pass and the power of man to persecute fellow man defeated, at least in this instance, though some countries still persecute them, but `Father Time' is the overall master in bringing about change.

Attempted suicide

Prior to the decriminalisation of suicide, there existed a small minority which made a *difference.* The one who attempted suicide and succeeded, was able to escape the penal law because he or she was beyond its reach. But the one who failed, was prosecuted for "attempted" suicide, which now is no longer an offence. A few British Christians became Muslim and joined the suicide bombers but suicide bombers kill innocent people as well as themselves and the killing of others is criminal – novel ideals defy the law until it is changed to suit novel situations. The growth of population breeds novel situations which may be regarded as criminal, depending upon the attitude of policy makers or legislators to address novel issues.

7 - WOMEN

"Not exclusively any more. I have left the door open", so said Nancy (Lady Astor, American born) when she was congratulated as first woman Member of Westminster Parliament in 1879. Since then the number of women who have entered that open door, compared to men, is unimpressive.

Though women have attained positions at the apex in occupations hitherto exclusive to men; but statistics show that a greater number of men than women are Members of Parliament as those holding apex positions. Nancy's statement was made 124 years ago and over a hundred years since the suffragette movement.

The Suffragettes were British women from upper and middle-class backgrounds, who strived to gap the *difference* between men and women on the vote as they struggled for change within society. Along with them were the advocates for woman's rights such as John Stuart Mill who first introduced the idea in 1865 to the British electorate.

Their efforts were enough to spearhead a movement drawing a mass of groups of women fighting for the right of women to vote. Nineteenth Century personages who championed women's rights included men such as John Bright and Richard Cobden while John Stuart Mill topped the bill. The first women's suffrage association was founded in 1865 :

"...the absorption of all [women's] rights, all property as well as all freedom of

action, is complete. The two are called 'one person in law', for the purpose of inferring that whatever is hers is his, but the parallel inference is never drawn

that whatever is his is hers...I am far from pretending that wives are in general

no bettertreated than slaves; but no slave is a slave to the same lengths, and in

so full a sense of the word, as a wife is."

- John Stuart Mill 1869.

The first literary composition in 1792 on the feminist ideology was perhaps Mary Wollstonecraft's A Vindication of the Rights of Woman in which she sought to persuade women to strive to acquire strength, both of mind and body, and to persuade them that the soft approach of heart, delicacy of sentiment and refinement of taste would be seen as a derisive weakness:

> *"It would be an endless task to trace the variety of meanness, cares and sorrows into which women are plunged by the prevailing opinion, that they were created rather to feel than reason, and that all the power they obtain, must be obtained by their charms and weakness."*

The nature of women's occupations has evolved with the changes affecting women generally. The goal has been for women to occupy positions previously exclusive to men. The system has altered to a great extent to accommodate women's demands but the changes have not suited every man's wish, the constant running thread in the archaic syndrome, the *status quo* – the *difference* still exists to an undesirable extent.

There is nothing dishonourable about the term 'housewife' save where some automatically assume it for every woman and stereotype her as such. The success of the husband in the public sphere lies in the strength behind him: the soft touch of woman, the wife. Even the German soldier in the Second World War following orders, subconsciously along with Allied soldiers, found solace in the song *Lilie Marlene* - because she gave him the stability he needed to get on with life whatever it presented. Over the years women strove to obtain the status of wife as the socially acceptable role for them. Since the break free ideology of the 1960s an increasing number of women have moved from the assumed norm and looked for other occupations making the desired goal of "wife" somewhat redundant. Others have attained positions at the apex in occupations hitherto exclusive to men, regardless of which their position remained as immutable as before the sixties. That was partly due to the woman's own volition, to fall into the *archaic syndrome* trap.

Take a look at the monarchs of Britain and we will find that during the reign of queens much had been achieved by Britain on the world stage. Perhaps men in various 'forces' and occupations were inclined to serve a queen best, or maybe there is some other latent reason. Under Elizabeth I Britain conquered the seas. The great age of exploration commenced in her reign which led to the foundations of the British Empire in the seventeenth and eighteenth centuries. Colonisation brought England into conflict with Spain, another colonising power at that time. Humphrey Gilbert (c.1537-83), and his half brother Walter Raleigh colonised the eastern coast of North America and were early advocates of American colonization, as Spain had already laid claim to much of South and Central America. Elizabethan England's emergence on to the world stage owed much to merchant ships and common seamen. The country's growing merchant navy and the experienced seafaring community enabled England to move on to the world stage for the first time.

In the era of Queen Victoria, Britain emerged as the most powerful trading nation in the world 's social and economic revolution in setting the pace in the process of industrialisation: mining of coal, minerals and other raw materials and the production of iron, textiles and manufactured goods. What had just began was an unrivalled industrial progress. Perhaps the greatest achievement of the Victorian era was the building of the railway network changing permanently both social patterns and the landscape of not only Britain but of the whole empire, particularly India and Africa. Along with this came the communications revolution of Steam & speed: the power of steam on land, like the steamship, the railway pre-dates the Victorian era. Steam locomotives were extensively used on colliery and quarry lines, particularly in the north east of England, and experimentally in other areas, during the first decades of the 19th century, with the technology being constantly improved by engineers such as George Stephenson and Richard Trevithick.

The Victorian era was an era of relative peace, population increase, material development, social reform, intellectual development in literature, with writers such as John Stuart Mill, Karl Marx, and new education in the rise of the novel in the books of Jane Austen, the Bronte sisters, Charles Dickens and others. The Victorian era was also one that ventured into the freedom of expression. Some ingenious personages emerged to express themselves in subtle language. This was demonstrated in literature; for example, the nursery rhyme below in its intrinsic political message:

Hush a bye baby on the tree top
When the wind blows the cradle will rock...
When the bough breaks the cradle will fall,
And down comes cradle, baby and all.

Perhaps there is no other era in British history, as the Victorian, on setting moral standards imposed by an iron fist particularly upon children; and the entrenchment of the *difference* between Us and Them.

Occupational segregation has been dictated by the institution of labour markets not only on gender but also on race and some other *difference,* a universal thread that weaves through social organisation; and which has had a negative effect on the labour market function and efficiency. Many a woman has toiled to bring up and educate sons, or brothers in some instances, to the professional class at the expense of her own advancement. This was because society gave opportunity to the male child as more deserving than the female child - gender *difference*. All taken for granted as the duty of the female, though there were few widowers who brought up children on their own without state benefit, unlike widows.

Retirement income through state encouragement of occupational and retail funds affect men and women differently where relative legal forms adopted in income privatisation assumes a forty-year continuous working life. Since women spent only half their working lives than men, substantial pension did not accrue to them. Unless they were married, in retirement most women had lived in real poverty, particularly if they did not own a home. For many decades places of employment accepted women but in a second class role to men even though some of them may have been as good or sometimes even better than the men. Women always ended hitting what came to be called the "glass ceiling". European Community law has to some extent addressed this disparity and influenced domestic law accordingly. Perhaps on this point one may say the travesty of EU law on domestic law balances itself out.

The first of a series of property Acts was passed in 1870 which gave married women the right to possess their earnings, but not any other right to property. For many decades this situation prevailed and woman accepted and in fact, lived in blissful ignorance of subjugation in the gender *difference*. Property rights have evolved along with women's rights. Normally the name on the title deeds was that of the owner of the property, though a spouse had the right to share the matrimonial home even if not named in the title deeds. For those who cohabited (without marriage) there was no such right. Women then always looked to marriage as a lifetime occupation because by marriage society accorded them a "respectable status." Where they failed to obtain the state of marriage they took to the wheel to spin wool or yarn for knitting garments and "spinster" entered the English dictionary. The term was then attributable to that type of woman, as her officially recognised occupation, both privately and formally on forms of any nature.

Socially, the married woman tended to look down upon the spinster as a "non-achiever"; for not all women promote the interests of other women. Premier John Major was the first to open the door to women in the exclusively male Cabinet of Westminster. Prior to Major, Premier Thatcher, in her cabinet there was not a single woman, but she chose to be surrounded by men who, in the end, ousted her.

A NEWSPAPER REPORTER USED THE PHRASE "petticoat power" in reporting on the first women members in the Cabinet. In describing the slight disorder that occurred that day, involving the public crowd around Westminster to witness the historical event, he said that a "police woman came forward to put things in order". And, that it was truly a 'woman's day!' The proficiency of journalists in their mastery of the English language in its descriptive usage and in grasping momentous situations, is commendable – but this reporter was enjoying his mickey on women and the novel *difference.*

The origin of this motif, "petticoat power", is *Women in British Politics,* 1760-1860: *The Power of the Petticoat*, edited by Kathy Glendale and Sarah Richardson. The meaning is that British women could highlight the motif of `petticoat influence' as a double edged sword to celebrate their influence and make a *difference* in politics as in the domestic sphere. The motif effectively demonstrated female influence in elections, emancipation of Jews among others. The domestic aspect of `petticoat power' was demonstrated by one of the most celebrated and beautiful film stars of the twentieth century, Elizabeth Taylor, in *Cat on a Hot Tin Roof,* though in the film the `power' had been temporarily frustrated.

More often than not men are threatened by women in apex positions and the disparity is world wide. The second class role of women applies universally. In the South African women's rugby team, Purple Hearts, a male player said:

"I don't mind women playing rugby, so long as they don't try to compete on equal terms with men."

In passing it should be noted that an African woman, prior to Westernisation, was physically stronger than man because she did all the manual labour without which she could not obtain a husband. However, like every situation there are advantages and disadvantages. The advantage in the African scenario, was her exquisite deportment from balancing heavy loads on her head. While European beauty therapists gave a pupil a book to balance on her head while walking!

If a woman succeeds in obtaining a profession she may be in danger of losing her man, the slightest *difference* becomes magnified and more likely than not the relationship would end. Unless the man was one who would support her. Acquiescence is sometimes taken for contentment where complacency is a disaster.

The goal has been for women to occupy positions previously exclusive to men. The system has altered to a great extent to accommodate women's demands but the changes have not suited every man's wish, particularly those who wish to preserve the *status quo.*

In both marriage and cohabitation, as in all human existence, the importance of a house as a home is vital. In modern 'partnership' (the modern terminology for cohabitation without marriage), there are two types of situations: those who share a house (usually the younger set with small children) and those who live in their own separate houses and meet in each other's houses on a sort of part-time basis.

The majority in the latter scenario are from middle age and beyond with grown up children. The revolutionary changes of the sixties created a situation leading to homelessness. Now it is over the top, women have double rights, the pill and the abortion on demand. There is a *difference* between abortion and miscarriage. In abortion there is an intention to destroy life, miscarriage is the unintentional loss of life. Some gave away their babies on the issue of `illegitimacy' – a *difference* between `married' and `unmarried'. Prestige of the family bastion in the state of marriage.

There is no such a thing as an illegitimate or orphan child in non-Western societies. There are always the grandparents, aunties and uncles to mind the child where it is natural to suckle a baby anywhere but in Western societies it is a taboo. Yet, some women, even in the Westminster Parliament, wear plunge neckline dresses/tops for reasons known to themselves: to be oneself, to cut a buxom picture, or to impress, but whom? There are seven billion of us on this planet, we cannot be all the same nor can we all want the same things - *difference* is creation's variety.

Starting in 2004, Forbes magazine has made a list of the 100 most powerful women in the world, edited by notable Forbes journalists and based on visibility and economic impact. Leading the table seven times in the last eight years Angela Merkel, Chancellor of Germany, said to be the world's most powerful woman. The list contains the fields of politics, philanthropy, business, technology, media, real estate, investments, fashion, research physics, food and beverages, and celebrity. Given the current population size of seven billion on our planet in 2013 the figure is minuscule, for every one job occupied by one woman there are one hundred men in similar occupations. Compare: for ten male billionaires there are only two women.

Within the past forty years the world has seen not only the emancipation of women but also of minority groups of various kinds: children, the disabled, recognition of self-determination of peoples in Africa and elsewhere; disintegration of apartheid in South Africa and many more. The change in the mode of economy was triggered by the Marxist conception in the freedom to job access; the sexual revolution in the myth of free love; the era of the collapse of social estates, and the break down of the bastion of social structure, the nuclear family. Despite the so-called changes by-gone ideals are still faintly alive today. Perhaps this may be attributed to the growth of population in the expansion of new, and retention of old, ideals, one person, one opinion. If you have a hundred people you have one hundred different opinions.

Marriage

From the post sixties contemporary society had increasingly derided the state of marriage. The traditional concept of marriage carried the legal stamp as the recognised prosaic enduring bastion of social structure common to and recognised by most cultures globally, albeit under different customs and laws. Most marriages bear the contractual characteristic. Any deviation from the traditional mode of union had been regarded as socially abnormal though increasingly tolerated but not accepted. Marriage had been undermined by partnership (hand-fasted), though this mode of union was in the minority. "Hand-fasted" is an archaic phrase and predecessor to cohabitation under Scots family law. A hand-fasted union, as the modern cohabitation, was legally recognised as a marriage by habit and repute, unlike cohabitation in England, no marriage no right.

It fits contemporary modern society in the individual's quest for security and happiness in a union which increasingly became a challenge to the long standing authority on marriage. The constant running thread since Genesis to the present day is the *archaic syndrome:* Protracted gestation in pregnancy bound woman to the home as the nurturer; while man had been more able to honour the social contract in occupation beyond procreation. Set norms remained immutable for a long time despite the rapid evolution of society. Since the beginning of time the *difference* between man and woman influenced the division of labour in functional existence.

This developed to the only occupations open to women: *housewife or spinster* or the oldest profession, *prostitution*. There is nothing dishonourable about the state of housewife. For years woman strove to obtain that status as the socially acceptable role for her. Since the sixties an increasing number of women chose to break free and looked to other occupations - a case for change versus stagnation.

On the history of the housewife in Britain the relations of gender have determined and classified the division of labour. The housewife over the years has been an unpaid worker, a latent support in the private sector. She has worn a number of hats for functional existence: cook, cleaner, children's nanny, dhobi (Urdu for laundryman) and other chores. Since the sixties men have done well in resigning themselves to domestic chores and some are excellent cooks. Sadly, since the rise of feminism a greater number of men fared badly under divorce, a complete swing of the pendulum.

Historically women strove to conquer the three stages: the suffrage; the glass ceiling; and the sexual saga. Women belong to a majority group but at the apex of professions share with ethnic groups as a minority. The history of marriage reflects constant redefinition over the years. The 1949 redefinition permitted marriage of the over-sixteen while in 1986 redefinition saw civil marriages. What was unthinkable for many years is the extension of marriage to same sex couples who want to make a public commitment in the presence of their families and friends – and in some cases co-religionists. The majority want to celebrate the marriage of lesbians and gay men. A big *difference* in the debate of the century involving most sections of society. In 2013 this latest redefinition became law – so much for the moralists!

Redefinitions do not undermine any existing or future marriages or their nature, at least for the moment, but Time is the master, and the evolution of society is inevitable. Shall judgmental attitudes focused on *difference* disappear by evolution for a more humanitarian society? People have married for political or economical alliances or other reasons and not always for love for the espoused. Though many marry for love or both love and position.

Since marriage may also be the first rung of a ladder to a monarch's throne, marriage carries some characteristics of a `social contract' rather than a `social covenant'. The *difference* is that the former carries commercial connotations and the latter is a moral bond. It is, of course, only until things go wrong that the contract aspect emerges and ugliness sets in to the sadness of a beautiful relationship that may exist between man and woman. The homosexual scenario has yet to prove itself on this point, but only Time can tell. In any co-existence togetherness, familiarity and proximity combine the essence of enjoyment in peaceful bliss but they can also be the agents of human conflict.

A thoughtless word may be misunderstood and seen as non-constructive criticism. The parties no longer trust each other and each feels that the other will deprive him or her of access to children and property, though the majority of husbands give up on their children, while some do not. Contempt then sets in to obliterate euphoria, arguments follow and increased stress levels, which fail to trigger the brain to the fusion of hormones. In such an environment *grace* departs and the contractual aspect of marriage sets in motion the legal machinery for settlement. Three aspects become paramount: financial cost, sometimes social ostracism and loss of contemporary friends and acquaintances who may find continued socialisation with either as an embarrassment.

Under the umbrella of marriage the wife's rights are protected as those of the children of the marriage in the settlement of custody/access to children and division of property, the most significant items in marriage in most cultures. But no one suffers more than the children who fall between two bickering parents on who will have what. Prince Albert, a man who enjoyed a blissful married life, said on the eve of his marriage to Queen Victoria:

"All tragedies are finished by death, and all comedies end by marriage."

The nuclear family of most Western Europeans societies, consisting of parents and children which has to some extent given way to the one parent family, a possible direct result of feminist ideology influence. One parent family consists of mother and child, though over the centuries mother was left with child, sometimes regardless of marriage. The extended family system includes parents, children, cousins, aunties, uncles, other agnates and affines, based on common grandparents and is common to the social structures of the Mediterranean and of non-Westernised cultures.

MARRIAGE IN BRITAIN had been a *difference* between public and private life. The public aspect was the state, politics, and the market, the sphere of man with absolute power over woman and children whereby inequalities of power between the gender and generations were moderated.

The inequalities of power arose due to the emancipation of the

Western European woman. The core of the private aspect was dedication embedded in the family, the sphere of the woman. The myth of privacy of a free and unencumbered family camouflages the fact that the private sphere is controlled by external factors of the public sphere:

"Wife and husband are one person and that person is the Husband."

Dictum of Judge Blackstone.

Prior to the sixties the power of women was concentrated in the domestic sector. The success or failure of many a man in the public sphere depended and still depends to some extent on the wife - the `petticoat power', or the wisdom behind the throne.

PATRIARCHAL AUTHORITY had been the prerogative of kings over the centuries in most cultures of the world. In fact, most social organisations commenced with a head man, or king, Britain; kaiser, Germany; tsar, Russia; rahaman, India; mfumu, Bantu; the shah of Iran, the list goes on... of head of a group of people in a given area as protector and fountain of justice.

Except societies without a leader or head (acephalous, medieval Latin from Greek *akephalos*: a = without + *kephale* = head) who are very much in the minority. Save matrilineal societies, where nonetheless, the head was/is male, the son of a sister. For succession purposes, maternity is provable while paternity had/has no proof in any society, until science gave us the technology of DNA.

THE CONCEPT OF LIBERTY, that is to say against the tyranny of political rule, like most ideals that sought to overthrow the old order, is a historical development in the evolution of human perception.

Political rule carried, and in some instances still carries, to a certain degree, the power to use patriarchal authority against the ruled to the same extent as against external enemies:

"Wherever there is an ascendant class, large morality of

the country emanates from its class interest, and its feelings

of class superiority." John Stuart Mill – *Utilitarianism.*

The power of ruler against the ruled was not confined to king and people or state and people, according to a male champion of the liberation of women, John Stuart Mill:

"The morality between Spartans and Helots, between

Planters and Negroes, between princes and subjects,

between nobles and roturiers [not noble birth]*,*

between men and women..."

Married women had no independent existence during marriage until 1882. The wife could not even own property. The man who married a woman with property did well for himself for the law gave him the right to own all of his wife's property in marriage. One of the duties imposed by marriage was to live together and the duty to support each other, and the right to adopt a child. Where the house was in the sole name of one spouse the other had the right of occupation. In cohabitation, without marriage, the other occupied the home by licence as any other visitor.

In criminal proceedings a spouse may have been compelled to give evidence for the defence unless he or she was a co-defendant and not for the prosecution, except where the spouse was a victim and the charge involved injury or certain connected offences; and wherethe offence was against a person under sixteen years of age. No such rules were imposed upon those who were not married to each other. Marriage as recognised on those legal rights, which called for certain formalities, mainly the need for witnesses and a public ceremony; the consequent effects of the abolition of the common law wife or husband concept of pre-1753.

For a number of reasons, such as to avoid secret marriages, in the case where one fell in love with someone out of their accepted social strata and consequences, and legal inheritance for the eldest son. Since 1753 the mode of marriage has been a church ceremony and the alternative, civil ceremony in the marriage registry office of a government department since 1836. There were no other alternatives to these two modes of marriage.

Many people mistakenly believe that by simply living together, the law could give one the same rights as marriage. Others believed that by having a child together they acquired legal rights, whether married, civil partnered, or not. In some instances in modern times there is the tendency to refer to unmarried couples as `common law' wife or husband particularly common law wife:

> *"There is no such a thing as a common law wife [or hushand] in English law..."* Lord Denning.

Whether it is the ancient espoused or the modern partnership some parties are in a monogamous union. Monogamy is a Christian concept of marriage. Given the number of married men in Christian societies who have extra marital relations, monogamy is truly a myth and a hypocrisy. Though, infidelity is by no means confined to the male species. Many-a-man has fathered a child who is not his, without knowing. The DNA test is concrete evidence of paternity but giving birth to a child in any society is primary evidence.

According to two experts on the subject of monogamy:

> *"Monogamy may be the rule, but it is not the practice – not even for animals."*

Since the emancipation of women and its consequent changes in marriage, divorce, and property laws, a wife became entitled to a half share of the husband's entire property. No marriage no right. Poetry and prose, in its historical and contemporary aspects, and other people's experiences, may give us only a glimpse of marital love. The rest is speculative assumptions, unless, one had the strength of Hercules to lift house roofs and peer within the enclosed walls. Because of the `private' nature of intimacy, it is difficult to accept the graphical details of sexual relations as portrayed on the screen and some find them offensive – nothing is kept private these days. The old films are only suggestive on this point leaving much to one's own imagination.

Divorce in British society and mimickers of British society stood in its own category and was once an absolute bar to marriage. Like everything else there are victims who get caught in the norms of particular historical eras. Some of the biggest divorce scandals (divorce-gates!) have involved the elite and above. Virtues and vices apply to all humanity regardless of rank. Transparency in more recent years has taken hold while in the past, because of lack of it, many things were hidden. Today divorce is no big deal and the *difference* between divorcee and non-divorcee is insignificant. Nonetheless, the prescriptions of social rules can be cruel:

"Society is a corrupting force that encourages the

individual to reject personal conscience for purposes

of the collective good"

- Khalil Gibran.

Since the rise of feminist power a greater number of men have fared badly under divorce, a complete swing of the pendulum. In his mind there is, not a type of woman, but the stereotype of all women. Not only is he bereft of his children, and possibly grandchildren, the designing woman is in control. She is an actress caught in the evolution of and has grasped the wrong end of emancipation. Media reports on real celebrity divorces have shown us this type of woman - who will attempt to skin her spouse alive, if given half a chance.

Marriage and family though shaken by the changes of the sixties remains an enduring bastion for a good number still. Find many a successful man and you can bet your bottom dollar that behind the success there is the intrinsic *grace* of a woman that calls for no militancy or masculine stamina. He hasn't a worry in the world save in running his business or profession; for she gives him the stability he needs within the bastion of marriage. The majority of men who make important decisions that affect the every day lives of women belong to the bastion of marriage. In the office, many a man will hide behind the skirts of his female assistant, while she is at the forefront furtively and eloquently muscling with his clients.

A friend once said:

"Husband and wife are like pot and lid, they fit".

Though I am uncertain, to this day, as to which is the lid! But the true liberation of woman lies in *economic independence* without financial aid and free from man. However hard she may work in their joint venture, some man will take all the credit and say that she was in a position of 'trust' for him.

Gender war

It has been said that the gender war commenced from what was called the permissive sixties, also called the sexual revolution, and the sexual liberation of women. A break-free and a challenge to the *difference* between the genders as a consequence of the emancipation of women. It has also been said that this was as an indirect result of the formal Assumption of the Virgin Mary into Heaven by the Catholic Church, Eastern Orthodoxy, Oriental Orthodoxy and other parts of Anglicanism.

One cannot help questioning the merits of this concept: innocence versus licentiousness? And, that consequently the assumption indirectly accelerated the voice of the feminist movement in the collective attitudes of women and progressed gradually reaching its peak in the nineteen-eighties. The irony is that in the so-called Christian countries, more so Roman Catholic, the Virgin Mary had been revered because she gave birth to a Saviour, yet at the same time the second class position of women was strongest in those areas. Gender wars as world wars, internal wars, political wars, and other wars regardless of their nature, commence and endure where there are opposing ideals, a *difference*. For the woman who accepted the *status quo*, and did not seek a personal identity, or was morally supported by the man who loved her there was no gender war. There are plenty of this latter-type of man out there, a role model for the twenty-first century. Apparent in the break-free ideology the advent of the pill as a reliable contraception and the relaxation of divorce laws were among the major responses to the sexual revolution. A revolution in the enhancement of individual expression which gave rise to free sex or free love, as some called it; and a subsequent pressure on the *status quo*. Rife was sexual rhetoric without which it was regarded as a psychological suppression.

Sexuality is a subject that triggered hot feminist debate from the late 1920s to the late sixties onwards, addressing the cultural, psychic mechanism that existed in the perpetual sexual inequality in Western European societies. The Masters and Johnson studies inferred that the young were sexually active, whereas the non-young were sexually inert; and that as most women grew older they were less likely to fantasise about sex. But man will vaunt on his sexual conquests, which are mere fantasies - wishful thinking turned to thoughtful wishing. The rise of feminism was linked with changes in the position of women. Significantly, the increase of married women in paid employment; the advent of legal aid and easily accessible divorce; increasing its rate; the rise of children born out of wedlock; and the consequent mother and child poverty. Despite that the pill gave women freedom without the fear of pregnancy. Fanatical bra-dumping was a useless gesture since the mammary is nature's inbuilt of the female anatomy. This may have led to the decrease of bra sales, and as a consequence to the collapse of the economy.

IT WAS SPECULATED that sperm may be threatened by possible obsolescence. The year 2010 by the advance of technology in genetic engineering research, made this speculation a reality: either of lesbian couples may incubate gen-rich to carry both their blood lines. But this would only create a *difference* in the novelty of a minority group. The University of Newcastle made a breakthrough in creating from a female human embryo for lesbian couples to have their own biological children from the bone marrow of a woman which could be used to fertilise an egg from her partner (BBC Radio4 22/04/13). The era of the designer baby is already yesterday's news. Perhaps what is to come is a choice of baby labels, as in fashion, coined by the supplier of the service or whoever. That sperm could be made obsolete by design was unthinkable. So, it was before homosexuality became decriminalised. Nonetheless, the traditional births by sperm and ovum are still very much in the majority.

By the Marriage (Same Sex Couples) Act 2013 homosexual marriage became a reality somewhat removing the *difference* between heterosexual and homosexual. If heterosexual traditional marriage was the best mode of union why is the divorce rate so high in the state of traditional marriage? This does not, of course, mean same gender marriages would be free from the strife some suffer in traditional marriages. Neither is it a guarantee against the problems of property division and custody of children at the end of the marriage, where children were begotten by the aid of modern technology or by adoption.

Perhaps the remarkable point is the fairness of any legal system that bows to the evolution of society, albeit slowly, to alter and protect situations which are not novel in themselves. Nonetheless, in this scenario for some who ask: where do ethics stand? The technology is also available to the gays who can have a baby with a surrogate mother. The first ever Britain's "Surrogacy Agency" baby centre opened in Danbury, Essex in February 2011 (*The Telegraph* and other media reports). The centre welcomes the needs of same-sex couples.

The idea of an all-female society is not new, however. In Greek mythology and Classical antiquity the Amazons were a group of all-female warriors. According to Herodotus, they existed in a region bordering Scythia and Sarmatia, modern territory of Ukraine. Other historians place them in Asia Minor, or more often Libya. Notable queens of the Amazons were Penthesilea, who participated in the Trojan War, and her sister Hippolyta. `Amazon' is a term for female warriors though now not strictly so. All the changes that have taken place in technology and legislation only add to the number of categories of *difference* in a greater variety of aspects.

SCIENCE PROVIDED EVIDENCE that every embryo-blast was female at conception up and until hormones 'kick in' when the Y and X chromosomes *differentiate* the male from the female. The embryo-blast may overture its own reality in the equality of male and female as humans and over-power the *difference.* A point further upon which woman may claim superiority over man. Though the supplier of the Y or X is the male. Yet, he also enters the world through the female, but the Creator knows all things. Given the circumstances of the emergence of the embryo-blast, every human being is a winner and an achiever in the sperm race, she out-raced fellow candidates to the ovum gate. However, the so-called civilising process by parental and social corrections, perfect according to them, remains the confusion of the offspring, particularly in adolescence.

In our world novelties never cease. A British woman married herself in November 2013 on a park bench at Westminster Parliament after being single for six years (*The Guardian*). She was inspired by Bjork's song:

"My name is Izobel, married to myself."

Grace Gelder decided to organise the wedding (*Mail on Line* 19/11/14). At the height of the technology era, highlighted are the "all boys" club and the "all girls club", in addition to which,

Grace initiated the "self club?" But it takes a number of people to form a 'club' – perhaps when the idea takes hold there shall be a good number of 'married to myself' individuals to form a club...

IN ANCIENT TIMES there was no knowledge about the connection between sex and procreation. When woman gave birth, "...they deduced that the world itself must have been created by a divine woman, the Great Mother, who was the universe itself". Woman grasped this legend to assert that women were superior to men because they incubate and give life. Then man retaliated:

"Who gave her the seed in the first place?"

The quest was and continues but to a lesser degree, as to whether the superior label should be pinned on man or on woman, and that both were entrusted with the mutual duty to rear their offspring was an assumption of social order. Not all children are reared by those who beget them. Man claims that he has 10-20 times more testosterone than woman, and that the hypothalamus of his brain is larger than that of woman. For many centuries society condoned the claim. Therefore, "promiscuity" and "tart" were terms applied to the female who was a mere flirt yet the male was seen as the mere flirt as man's indiscretions had been socially condoned.

"Man loves woman with carnal desire...and for the physical enjoyment he can get with her and not because she is a human being like himself" (Tolstoy). So, the 'ping pong' went on. In non-Westernised societies where divorce was rare the 'ping pong' was considered taboo.

Now it is not possible to pin-point the precise moment of conception of a human being. Due to modern technology the traditional concept contains a fundamental ambiguity. This is due to the culling of unsuitable embryos, the freezing of others, and the testing of embryos for genetic abnormalities. The legal status of these novel situations would depend on the point in the process of conception chosen to trigger appropriate laws. Now conception is a forty-eight hour process during which the haploid genomes of the sperm and egg gradually and precisely transform into the functioning genome of a new human embryo.

Some men find it difficult to distinguish between partner and wife, whether he is looking for a girl friend (a misnomer for the geriatrics) or a girl Friday in his search for the comforts provided for by a wife but without the cost of keeping a wife. A case for *moral bondage* on the part of woman versus the *status quo*. In the culmination of the gender war its idealism was diminished by gender selection which motivated some abortions in favour of boys once the gender of the foetus was known (BBC on "The Missing Girls"). The media and literature had generally informed that teen-age pregnancies in the Western world, where Britain topped the bill, were rife and that there were numerous botched up abortions outside the legal confines.

DIVISION OF LABOUR evolved in early human tribes and created two genders urgently dependent on one another with equality in importance. The human male has had a great impact beyond any human life as a destroyer of natural features and in the construction of artificial ones. Imagine, in every job on the Western culture side of our planet has been done by the male to the insignificance of all other species, by brain and not brawn (Morris). By this brain and not brawn attitude man has raped Mother Earth, by mining for gems, fuel and various. In less than one hundred years, fauna and flora of the earth has diminished to frightening proportions. Man has raped Mother Earth in the indulgence of natural resources. Talk of the advanced technology in extraction of shale gas commercially, known as fracking, is yet another blow on Mother Nature. Man has not taken blood from the veins of Mother Earth but from the arteries of her blood – what does the future hold for Mother Earth and all that dwell on her?

VISIT THE MAGISTRATE'S court (England) or the Sheriff's court (Scotland) to observe preliminary criminal hearings. You would be horrified, nay distressed, to find that the vast majority of offenders are *male* between the ages of eighteen to twenty-eight. On a certain hearing, a mother, occasionally dubs a white handkerchief to her wet eyes, sitting beside and holding the hand of her physically fit twenty-eight year old son. He had been accused of stealing and selling the tyres of his father's Jaguar car. She lets go off his hand for the charge to be read to him. What has Western society done to the male child?

The male forefront exertion in all things may be seen as residual in risk-taking sports that men engage in, though a lesser number of women have been added to the list as in other occupations. From ancient to present the seed scattering strategy belongs largely to the male. However, DNA paternity testing (1955/6 without need of the courts) in a 1998-2004 report, sixteen out of every one hundred children proved to be children of men who were not husbands of their mothers. The gender war existed in all social strata as can be seen in the following quote from the top shelf, Nancy Astor to Winston Churchill at a dinner party:

"Winston, if you were my husband, I would poison your coffee!"

To which Winston replied:

"Madam, if I were your husband I would drink it!"

8 - SEXUALITY AND GENDER

Charles Perrault (1628-1703) French author first published *Sleeping Beauty* among others from pre-existing folk tales, about a beautiful young woman (`girl' is often not appropriately used for young woman) depicting sleeping as the `overt' aspect, while the `covet' is the arousal of sexuality by the handsome Prince. *Sleeping Beauty* and *Prince Charming* have been adapted in a variety of entertainments. Sexuality and gender has had its share of evolution, in tandem with gender wars, culminating in the Marriage (Same Sex Couples) Act 2013. Homosexuality had been abhorred while the extremist moralist killed them for their choice of sexuality. Like everything else where there is a *difference* there is conflict in varying degrees – there is still a great number that finds homosexuality abhorrent because there is a *difference* with heterosexual.

THE POST SIXTIES was riddled with sex ignorance and irresponsible sex. This did not only affect the feminist history but alongside with the mode of economy, triggered by the Marxist conception of class and power politics. Also as the era of the collapse of paternalism, social estates, and the break down of the bastion of social structure, the nuclear family. From the late 1950s, when people from the colonies sought education in Britain, in London's Hyde Park the amusing incidents were from the novelty of black men embracing blond white women on the beautiful lawns to the soap box at Speaker's Corner, home of free speech without the fear of defamation – a place once used for public executions. Sexuality then fell into two major views apparent in its contemporary behaviour: the pre-sixties and the post-sixties. Both views exhibited a degree of ignorance and dwelt on speculative sex. The former view regarded sex as unwholesome and horrible to which only the married man and woman could claim a right for the purpose of procreation. And, supposedly sex was enjoyed only by loose women. Or for the single man regardless of whom he made pregnant. Also masturbation was regarded as taboo. Yet, regardless of rank, life is sexually transmitted where the conceived have no choice.

Sexual rhetoric extended to sexual preferences and derision of types and comparisons: the German lover as sharing the formality of the Continental Johnnies; the lousy Italian lover; we heard less about the French - they had it down to a fine art by their mistresses culture and by their celebrated motif: *Vive la difference!* Not that non-French did not have mistresses – the *difference* was that the French were and still are less hypocritical about it. Be that as it may. tt was said that courtly love was invented by medieval Britons and poetry and prose reflected this aspect.   At the same time portraying the Englishman as inept – but we see the growth of the English population. Regardless, he is celebrated by Ertha Kitt in her song: *An Englisman Takes His Time*. And, many other derisions, mere speculations on sex as a game in the myth of female chastity and the social condonation of male promiscuity. The force of sexual preference is the myth of love.

"Love lives in perpetuity but dies upon touching" (Hardy). The dying is caused by the touching without 'grace' of the mind to complement the anatomy, of course. All is part of what the English are good at: laughing at themselves. Physical impotence may be the only one that is a medical condition, rather than psychological impotence. Sexuality is a combined condition of the mental and physical aspects. *Fantasy* is the psyche and sex begins in the mind. A failure or lack of appropriate fantasy applies to both men and to women, though there is a general assumption that impotence applies only to man. The *difference*

is one of genitalia more evident in man because of his extroverted genitals: *vive la difference* as the romantic heterosexual Frenchman puts it (misinterpreted by some men to mean superiority of man over woman). Adverse factors blur the psyche and causes the lack of fusion of mind and body, leading to sexual incompatibility, the defrauder of youth and breeds frustration. The war of sexes rages and the gender gap widens into a breakdown of *friendship*, the bedrock of all kinds of relationships. Pecuniary embarrassment also glooms the spirit in the inevitable punctiliousness of daily living and the necessity of a *house* as a home. Fantasy abounds in its varieties of preferences and is as unique as each individual, though two people or a number of persons may share a common sexual fantasy.

BEFORE THE FEMINIST MOVEMENT the bunny was created, the ultimate fantasy medium, the abstract aspect of sex. It was the sex object by choice, featured in the Playboy Magazine; a somewhat mimicry of the Oriental Geisha (Japanese), the perfect hostess. The Bunny performed in Playboy Clubs of London's May Fair. Clad in petty sexually powerful costume to amuse and arouse the playboy and the psychedelic patterned garb to delight the big playboy. Her environment set a breakthrough in racial equality to some extent. She was recruited from all ethnic backgrounds, except black, between the ages of eighteen-twenty-one. Good looks and intelligence were the vital qualifications to display her body in dignity and limousine lifestyle. Selling professional sex to a strictly male clientèle but sex was no big deal, somewhat analogous to the strip-teaser. For the Bunny it was a means to an end upon which to build her own little empire on Bunny money. She fed the sexual fantasies of the male and many a wife owed her a debt of gratitude, unwittingly, for saving her marriage.

IN SOCIETIES AROUND THE WORLD a woman's breasts transcend all the cultures as the all time major "turn-on." In other societies the infant may be suckled anywhere, any time. In Western societies adults eat in public but not the little baby because man has turned woman's breasts into a fantasy. In most languages of the world without any apparent connection "mama" is the term for mother instinctively. Sexual activity in whatever form of preference if done covertly between consenting adults, causes no harm to any one and does not shock the precept of others, may receive the *live and let live* stamp.

Only thinking makes other people's preferences seem perverse. High profile public figures' indiscretions is delicious gossip highlighted by the media. The obsession to drag delicious gossip into the public arena is rife in the United Kingdom and the United States. European, African and the Oriental continents are less obsessed with this kind of adolescent attitude. One would reasonably expect that a man's infidelity was a matter between himself and his wife, more so his wife's concern.

The individual's perception of the concept of Eros was conditioned from early childhood by an established system of law and order in two-dimensional principles, under the reality and beyond the reality (Freud).This view indicated that law and society imposed rules of morality upon individuals. Though it is unclear as to whether morality is a subject that could be legislated. This leaves open the question as to how far our existence is improved by the imposition of rules of morality, and whether morality applies only to matters sexual.

According to one writer, Leonardo Da Vinci captures the aesthetic beauty and division of the mother and lover figures in the face of La Gioconda ("the jocund [happy] one", famously known as Mona Lisa. The man who is unable to distinguish the dividing line has not yet left his mother's womb. Everything we touch, see, feel, hear, or eat conjures up a form in our mind (Plato's theory of forms).

Perhaps one of the most truthful statements that may put paid to literature on the attempts of some in the race to educate people on sexuality, and the enduring myth and social taboos surrounding sex was that made by Kinsey:

"There is nothing more characteristic of sexual response than

" The fact that it is not the same in any two individuals."

The big question may be why are people so hang up about sexuality, particularly some Christians on homosexuality? There is nothing in the Bible to say that anyone would suffer for the sins of another, save that:

"...judge not, lest ye be judged."

Also, some women and some men who have passed middle-age and have no sexual partners regard other people's sexual activity as delicious gossip. As some church leaders who consider themselves to be the judges of morality, while some of their colleagues sexually abuse children. But discriminatory attitude usually extends to most minority groups or wherever there is a *difference* of any kind. What is a novel change is `transparency' in the whole of modern society and freedom of the media to highlight almost everything that happens in our daily existence. This leaves the question: Do we need a free press or a restricted one? The answer may be: certainly a free press but less 'intrusive'.

Perhaps this is the realisation of George Orwell's `Big Brother' watching you in his book *Nineteen Eighty-Four*. Orwell was predictive about the impingement on the freedom of citizens by government, the desirable, undesirable to some, effects of modern technology. Everything is good but it all depends on in whose hands it is.

Sexual abuse is both physical and emotional harm done to a child as a result of sexual relationship with an adult. The phrase can also be applied generally with reference to adult victims of molestation, incest or rape. But generally abuse is not confined to sex but also to rob a child of the innocence of childhood and this can come in different forms. Girls had been the victims, not only in household chores but sometimes forced into child labour; either because of the father's drinking habits or the mother's insatiable desire "to buy things" or both, among other reasons.

THE PRE-SIXTIES REGARDED SEX as unwholesome to which only the married man and woman could claim a right for the purpose of procreation. This view was much conditioned by Victorian attitudes; and the hypocrisy of this view lay in the fact that not only the single man, regardless of whom he made pregnant, got away with it. Particularly in the year of revolution 1968, the challenge to authority, the New Radical Left, in the mass demonstration on the war in Vietam through London's Oxford Street and Whitehall. The post sixties was a period of good middle class politics. Sadly this era saw the end of national service for young men, when young women ought to have been included in the national service. The passing of the London Season, the coming out of daughters as débutantes, the vehicle to marriage alliances to the upper class, for both men and women; and the rise of the lower strata in the collapse of social estates. The era when the world had seen not only the emancipation of women but also of minority groups of various kinds: children, the disabled, recognition of self-determination of peoples under European powers around the world. All former categories of eunuchs under overall patriarchal protection within the changing face of the hybrid class system.

The post sixties manifested in a great number of things towards a more open society. There is no doubt that change was apparent in a great number of things towards a more open society.

It was the heyday of youth power, the rise of pop music with names such as David Bowie, the Rolling Stones, the Beatles, and others in music and lyrics which truly reflected its own era of openness; of mini skirts and close-fitting sweaters, petticoats and stockings, Levis on women; the popularity of London's Carnaby Street and much more.

The breakdown of the bastion of social structure, parental protection, and the end of *something to come home to*. This was the beginning of homelessness. The consequences of leaving home and parental protection as highlighted in the film *Cathy Come Home* which drove home, to public awareness, of homelessness. Others made it to own a home but most did not. To fight a *difference* is courageous but it has its consequences.

The sex revolution escalated to the stage where sex had increasingly become a saleable commodity, through the media, such as television programmes, tabloid newspapers and other literature, for the gratification of both men and women. Served on a platter on the market square (cheapside, if you like!). Patriarchal protection was not a bad thing for its own era. Prior to the emancipation of women and black people, without patriarchal protection, life would have been unthinkable. Most things are right for their own particular time. Nonetheless, thank Heaven for the era of the myth of 'free love', the true cudgel that put paid to the use of the terms 'illegitimate' or 'bastard' for one born out of wedlock. Pejorative terms now directed at another in some outburst of frustration.

9 – CHILDREN

A baby does not have a choice as to how he or she is conceived or going to be reared: two parents, single parent whether within or without wedlock, heterosexual, lesbian or gay, upper, middle or lower class or royalty. In adulthood one may weed out certain aspects of childhood conditioning and find one's own identity. In the first place, no person ever asked to be conceived and every adult was once a child. Those who give birth to them do not always rear children and children are regarded in many different ways by adults. Perhaps of all differences the *difference* between child and adult is the deepest and appears to be less apparent, when one observes the attitude of some adults towards children. Though some say of the childless that the gods had not favoured them.

Ancient peoples prayed for a child to the Ibis, relative of the stork's procreative powers, a custom originating with the Turtons. The Celtic peoples believed that the stork ferried babies to people's homes. In ancient England, Germany and Scandinavia and other European countries, people believed that by the mere flight of the stork above their homes women would be impregnated with child. Some great men such as Socranus of Euphesus, Greece, in the fifteenth century CE advocated literacy for the midwife in order that she understood the importance of baby's safe delivery in comforting the labouring mother.

A baby is received differently by different people and for many centuries the male child had been more favoured than the female child. In China baby girls were killed at birth. This tendency can be seen where modern technology is used to select gender of foetus, leading to abortion if the gender is the undesirable one.

Some babies were killed at birth in other societies other than the Chinese, as deformed babies were and are still killed at birth in other societies. In most societies the birth of a baby is a joyful wondrous event regardless of gender. For some, there is family planning and for others babies are conceived by accident.

Some are born out of wedlock and others not. In some instances children become wards of the State. Most children know their mothers though they do not know their fathers. For some s/he is `nobody's child'.  Others `everybody's child'. Or `somebody's child'. In rare cases puberty descends upon them when mere toddlers. Some are hated by their mothers from the moment of birth for being female or mother has post-natal blues or other reasons. On a TV therapy programme in helping a mother to cope with her own baby she hated from birth, the infant sensed that she was hated and her natural strategy was to turn away from the mother's face. The sentience that is with us from the moment of conception. Yet the baby gave a sweet smile to the therapist in response to love and care.

In some countries, such as Brazil, street children were hated to the extent of being killed by death squads, and forced into the sewers to escape and survive. Children in many societies had and are still discriminated against because of the difference from adults and for some more than necessary suffer benign apartheid. In most things that may go wrong for adults, throughout the world, such as the separation of parents, poverty, wars, famine and many others, children suffer the most.

In the status of child there is a *difference* and the treatment of children is not always desirable. In certain societies adults eat first and the children eat what is left over. Watch television programmes on child poverty such as Save the Children and you will observe that the child is emaciated while the mother holding the child is not.

The mind cannot dispense what it has not first absorbed, and yet, some children rise above the *difference* between deprivation and privilege to self-taught. They aspire to levels above some privileged children and beyond the societies in which they were born into.

Illegitimacy had always been stigmatized in English Society. Since the 17th and the 18th centuries, the negative attitude was evident in legislation which denied them assistance from the poor rates. In Victorian England in 1834 the Poor Laws were reformed. The Bastardy Clause absolved the supposed father of any responsibility for the child. This move socially and economically victimized the mother in engineering the restoration of female morality. This led to a murderous form of institution known as 'baby farming' which preyed on infants of the humiliated and alienated mothers. Despite the tremendous toll it took on the lives of innocent children, the Victorians' fear of government intervention into social reform and the Victorian ideal of the inviolability of the family prevented its reform until the end of the 19th century.

Prior to the sixties a child born out of wedlock presented `illegitimacy' and a social stigma, what was then considered an undesirable state of affairs for the so-called good name of the family and society. The upper class used clinics to abort. Those born had to be abandoned by their mothers to be adopted by those not favoured by the gods. Could there be anything worse than a mother having to give up her child (or lose her child by death)? The death of loved ones strikes terror in our heart and permanently alters and diminishes our existence - I will never smile again till I smile at you...

A woman who had custody of their infant in a divorce in the mid-fifties said that as a single parent there was no *difference* between her and an unmarried mother. She was wrong. Had her baby been born out of wedlock she would not have been as welcomed by the family and society generally as she had been. Such was the state of morality then. In non Western societies there is no such a thing as an illegitimate or orphan child and in Africa it takes a village to rear a child. Where a mother may hate her baby the situation may not even become apparent because of the many who mother the baby, as the situation would become naturally rectified.

Over the centuries children have been born out of wedlock and they have become famous people performing great deeds which have lived through the centuries:

Confucius (CA551-479 BC), among his many quotes is:

"What you do not want done to yourself, do not do to others".

Not unlike what Jesus said:

"Do unto others as you would wish them to do unto you."

Leonardo da Vinci (1452-1519), great Italian artist, engineer and scientist; Lawrence of Arabia (1888-1935); William the Conqueror; Pope Clement VII; Henry Fitzroy (Fitzroy means son of king); Gabriella Bonheur, one of the world's greatest fashion icons popularly known as Coco Chanel, the list is endless. And, at least more than half of the entire seven billion of the world's population today were born out of wedlock.

BBC News (08/04/16) carried the article that the Most Reverend Justin Welby, Archbishop of Canterbury, discovered that he was the son of Sir Anthony Montague Browne (Sir Winston Churchill's last private secretary). The Archbishop had said a DNA test result revealing the identity of his real father had come as a 'complete surprise'. He had believed that his father was Gavin Welby (whisky salesman who died in 1977). Lady Williams of Elvel (the Archbishop's mother) confirmed she had a 'liaison' with Sir Anthony just before she wed in 1955.

There are many great people today in our modern times, who were born out of wedlock, some are billionaires and make a great contribution to the lives of many, and their outstanding deeds are of great inspiration to others. In a form of snobbery, the terms "illegitimate" or "bastard" were and are used by people who never bother to ask the most important question: "Does the seed have any control over its conception as a human?"

By the power of Time, child illegitimacy is now no longer a big deal but there is still a snobbish hangover by some. At one point the accusing finger had moved to whether or not gays or lesbians were fit people to foster children, without evidence of child abuse, but based on a so-called morality. A good number of heterosexuals have been known to murder and abuse children and yet the finger points at gays and lesbians who have not been known to murder children. Yet, there are children who by accident of circumstances are brought up by one person, man or woman, predominantly in the latter, gay or lesbian, but this presents an aspect of minority. In Britain in 1987 twenty-three percent of babies were born out of wedlock to those in cohabitation relationships. Gay and lesbian parents registered sixty-eight percent births and since January 2006 the homosexuals as a couple may adopt a child.

There is a general assumption that most men do not care for

their children when the union with the child's mother has soured. A good number of men love and feel for their children but the odds have been against them and some give up easily while others do not. It is easier to conceive than to rear a child and the responsibility of rearing the human child is a reality.

The human being carries the instinctual sense perception from the moment of conception. If that were not the case sperm would not instinctively strive to outrace fellow candidates to the ovum gate. From the moment of conception we are sentient. The essence of our being is the state of consciousness. Awareness and consciousness is a combined functional and inextricable whole and the ever-intrinsic presence of the self or ego.

According to anthropologists, at birth awareness combines the other part of our perception which is two-dimensional: the classification of the natural world, one's perception of natural surroundings such as the earth, sky, light of day, dark of night, atmosphere, space, surface of the ground and others. The other aspect is the social conditioning of the cultural world. From the moment of birth the infant's mind will absorb, by mimicking. Observe a baby trying to mimic things other people were doing around her, such as rubbing hands together; a habit some people have when they are talking within the home as out. From the moment of birth babies are watching and mimicking.

Babies are more observant than adults because they have an `initial' intellectual curiosity. As the days pass they get better and better at mimicking: actions, sounds, facial expressions and body language accompanied with baby jargon. Leave two babies by themselves and they will converse in their own social interaction.

What he or she can see around including the conditioning by

society:

"Give me the child until he is seven and I will give you the man" - St Francis Xavier. We all are mimickers (or plagiarisers, if you like) in all we do, there is nearly always a precedent for some knowledge, followed by some action.

The Bible teaches that we are born with sin but we carry the history and shortcomings of the society in which we were born The suppression of the individual's instincts from infancy prevents individual instinctual development and social conditioning is a questionable reality set over the centuries. We are ignorant of any possible alternatives in the world we have been taught to know.

Dr Jaroslav Koch of Prague believed and proved that if children were allowed to develop in their own way they would and made incredible strides; and that children are retarded by social prescriptions and conditioning. The majority of infants are capable of great feats and sensory perception begins with babies, they can see colours, feel things around them. We hear of the child protégé who has aspired to some great achievement at a very early age. This is because there has been a parent or some adult who has recognised and encouraged the child's natural instincts.

The general tendency by most parents is to adopt an ownership stance over children beyond the protective duty. The anthropologists (Durkheim and Mause) say society believes that the human mind lacks the innate capacity to construct complex systems of classification and the model for the arrangement of ideas is society itself. First we have to extricate ourselves from social conditioning before we can evolve into what we wish to be (Redfield). Childhood experiences have profound consequences in later life. Children are vulnerable because of their need for a sense of trust. The effects of psychological damage to the male child abused by the female are as lasting as those of the female or male child who has been sexually abused by a male. Most children who have been sexually abused in adult life become promiscuous, because practical sex had been impressed upon a tender mind.

The adult woman who takes advantage of a vulnerable male child in playful sexual seduction may escape offence unlike the male abuser. Her sexual organs are introverted and feature less prominently. Some men when toddlers have been abused by women.

As in most instances of child abuse the act is covert because it is committed by the least expected and the vulnerability of the child in which they take place - one form of *irresponsible* sex by the adult. The *difference* between the adult and the child in the latter is not capable of consent, the power of the performer over the object. But there are more men than women who abuse children.

The crime of rape had been against women, now it is extended to men, where there has been no consent. There are more men than women who abuse their daughters. Where the father sexually abuses their daughter the majority of mothers invariably turn a blind eye and in some cases the mother and daughter end up as rivals over him. Where the mother sexually abuses their son the husband is likely to be violent to the wife. Such is the dominance of the male over the female.

THE INDUSTRIAL REVOLUTION spelled economic freedom, so history has taught us to believe, but for whom? The *difference* between United Kingdom industrialists and the worker is reflected in the long working hours in the factories stretched to the extreme; and limited by the physical strength of the workers, particularly women. Daniel Dafoe describes his visit (1726) to the mills in the Calder Valley (north of England) where he observed hand loom weavers always busy carding and spinning: "no hands being unemployed from the youngest to the ancient". Children from age five worked in factories. The under fives were chained to machines while their mothers worked on the machines, for the children's safety. The factory women learned by necessity to `lip read' each other in communication because the machines were so noisy speech was out of the question. Iniquitous working conditions for European workers and forced labour from Africa were linked to the Industrial Revolution. Wealth and success at the enslavement of others? Compare with the twenty-first century: Children are still being exploited in a different way (BBC World News 29/7/13) by societies other than British. The FBI launched "Operation cross-Country" conducted under the "Innocence Lost" initiative on a 72-hour nationwide operation targeting pimps who preyed on children ranging from thirteen to seventeen years old and the youngest victim of nine years old resulting in the arrest of 150 pimps. Most of the children were found to have no concerned family members. The victims consisted of various racial backgrounds.

First, they were groomed to fill the void of lack of family concern about them. The FBI reported rescuing 2,700 children since 2003. Today, in the twenty-first century, we have the Rotheram (England) scandal of 1,400 children subjected to appalling sexual exploitation between 1997 and 2013 – while authority was basking. Others have followed this pattern on a larger scale.

We may put this to the passage of Time to bring us to the milestone of transparency; as contained in the Bible, Luke 8:17

and Ecclesiastes 12:14:

"For nothing is hidden that will not be made manifest, nor is

anything secret that will not be known and come to light...For

God will bring every deed into judgment, with every secret

thing, whether good or evil."

It appears that in any time of human existence on this planet there has always been those who will enslave others for their own ends. Black skin had been equated with labour. Regardless of their status, all children are conditioned to realise the aspect of *difference* as a way of life. Some who have experienced hard times, especially poverty in childhood, become `social conscious' and seek to improve the lot of children to make a *difference*. Some ignore the *difference,* determined to improve their own lot and strive to climb to a higher strata. We cannot all be the same, *difference* in perception: philanthropist versus conservative.

Education

The *difference* between the rich and poor is apparent in the evolution of the history of education. Prior to the eighteenth century education was not available to the children of the poor in WesternEurope. The notion of `compulsory' schooling for every child in every town from age six or seven, had not been envisaged then. In Britain the Industrial Revolution required the masses to be educated because industrialists wanted and believed that workers could keep records of production sales.

This service was then a task carried out by travelling workers from France, Germany and other countries. One of the last areas in Europe to adopt a compulsory system of education was England. The professions of doctors, engineers and such like were confined to the upper class.

Plato is credited for having popularized the concept of compulsory education in the Western world (The Republic, 380 BC, the definition of justice and the just man). Parents in Judaea in ancient times were required to teach their children informally. As cities, towns and villages developed Rabbis evolved. From the first century formal Jewish education was instituted in schools in every town and was made compulsory for children from the age of six or seven. The Aztec Triple Alliance (1428-1521) in what is now central Mexico is considered to be the first state to implement a system of universal compulsory education. In Scotland universal education began in 1561. In Western Europe mandatory primary education was introduced by Empress Maria Theresa of Austria in 1774.

The first time England and Wales became involved with education was from 1883 when the Westminster Parliament voted sums of money each year for the construction of schools for children of the poor. From medieval times the Church provided education to all classes of society in monasteries, at public schools, orphanages, charity schools, grammar schools, church foundations or by the chaplains to private households. By the late nineteenth century all university fellows and schoolmasters required to be in holy orders. Schoolmistresses taught the three 'Rs': reading writing and rithmatic, what we now know as arithmetic, in schools, charity schools and informal village schools.

The Church of England resisted early attempts for the state to provide secular education and church schools remained in the state school system. The practice of churches providing universal education was exported to the colonies for the education of the indigenous, which was not the concern of the imperial government. School was not free and attendance was not compulsory. Now, it may be an offence not to send a child to school since the passage of the Education Act 1998 and various legislation raises a penalty for failing to send a child to school in the form of a fine and/or imprisonment. The use of the powers was endorsed by the Education Secretary who believed it would send a message to irresponsible parents that they would be punished for damaging their children's education.

Only the elite were eligible to university education and the Oxford University is the mother of universities in Britain, established before 1167 followed by Cambridge in 1209. In Scotland, Universities were established in the early fifteenth and sixteenth centuries. By the late nineteenth century most cities of UK had a university. Polytechnics were formed in the expansion of higher education in the 1960s. After the passage of the Further and Higher Education Act 1992 they became independent universities awarding their own degrees; when the designation 'polytechnic' was dropped.

In recent years much emphasis has been placed on faith schools. A faith school in the UK teaches a general curriculum but with a curriculum that has formal links with a religious organisation. Such schools are funded by the state and may give priority to applicants who are of the faith of the school but they must also admit other applicants. Further, they are required to ensure that they comply with the School Admissions Code. The fair admissions campaign wants to ban the selection of pupils on the ground of faith in state schools of England and Wales. The new group says religion-based admission policies can fuel segregation and cause "distrust and disharmony". A Catholic Education Service spokeswoman rejected the claim that Catholic schools are socially divisive, while the British Humanist Association, the Accord Coalition and the Centre for Studies on Inclusive Education, asserted that a faith-based admissions system may have an adverse effect on communities. The House of Commons warned New Labour in 2001 against faith schools and its implications and yet the government proceeded to introduce the Education and Inspections Act of 2006. Faith schools are fertile ground for benign apartheid which in extreme cases may lead to problems, particularly at a time when the majority are seeking a society with fewer *differences*.

Poverty and discrimination is getting further entrenched along ethnic and religious lines and the Joseph Rowntree Foundation report indicated that tackling deprivation was more vital.

Many people from the British dependencies were hungry for and sought education in Western Europe particularly Britain. Prior to the independence of colonised areas foreign students were most welcome in Britain. Students on arrival in the United Kingdom observed the *difference* between the Britons of UK and those who lived in the colonies. The English and the Scots were more friendly and approachable than the colonists with the absence of the 'snobbery' seen abroad. By the time they returned home, after completion of their studies, they carried the impression that the people of Britain were 'incapable of cruelty'.

Twenty or so years after the independence of colonised areas the number of foreign students was on a much larger scale. While universities were more than ready to accept fees, almost twice higher than that paid by national students, from the foreign students the reality had its own difficulties. Most of the host country students were struggling with the novelty of the *difference* between themselves and the foreign students particularly the racial aspect and `excluded' them from their study groups.

In study groups the sharing of information simplified the task of study and foreign students had to rely on sheer merit for a pass. But then even this was not without drawbacks but the novelty also affected some of the tutors. Consequently the foreign student's merits would have had to be met with a tutor who was not racially prejudiced in order to get a pass or a higher mark.

Tutors hold `discretion' which is a form of `absolute power' in the granting of certificates or degrees and as most of us know absolute power corrupts absolutely. The next hurdle for the foreign students who had the right to live in Britain was to find a job placement which was riddled with the barriers of race and colour and in some instances ageism and sexism. Recently higher education institutions take `middle class' applicants to boost their income rather than take traditional 'British' students from deprived backgrounds who are likely to drop out (BBC Radio4 11/08/13). `Class' creeps back in here and there based on *difference* in values.

Poverty

That by any standard there is very little poverty in Britain today is debatable. Nonetheless, poverty is found in most countries of the world in varying degrees. The definition of poverty is political and contradictory which makes the measurement and alleviation of poverty difficult. Social exclusion has always existed but it became formally identified with poverty and poverty has remained immutable while the social label attached to poverty is in constant change. There had been much rhetoric debate among politicians and academics on the measurement of poverty focused on the question as to whether the function of Social Security (SS) should prevent want at the poverty level or rescue those below it. The welfare of parents affects children. In the UK a welfare state was first envisaged by the Royal Commission into the operations of the Poor Laws of 1832. It was found that the old poor law and English poor laws were subject to widespread abuse and criminality by its recipients in comparison to those who received private charity.

By the efforts of Benjamin Seebohm Rowntree and Charles Booth, social reformers of the nineteenth century, it was seen that at least one third of the population in the United Kingdom were living below the poverty line.

Since 1940 socialist and conservative ideologies had focused on the alleviation of poverty. The principles of less-eligibility whereby benefits had been assessed at the lowest labour-wage it dominated government policy from the Poor Law to new Labour. The principle operated in line with the null idea of state dependency by the destitute. The SS within the welfare state had evolved through three significant stages of reform: the Beveridge Report of 1942 which laid the foundations for the modern welfare state on matters such as the establishment of a National Health Service; in 1948 the National Insurance Scheme was implemented by the Labour government; and the changes of 1980-1990 addressed some of the Beveridge shortcomings, and the outgoing government proposals on the 'welfare to work' policy which had been followed to a large extent by new governments.

The improvement of the standard of living of the masses is a socialist ideology. The Labour electoral success in July 1945 was a peaceful revolution, the most Labour achieved was the welfare state. The horrors and deprivation of the Second World War was momentum in a hope for the future.

As early as 1940 a famous editorial in *The Times* stated:

> *"If we speak of democracy...equality...we do not speak of a*
>
> *political equality nullified by social and economic privilege.*
>
> *We speak of economic construction..."*

At least sixty percent of British society believed that the absolute standard of subsistence level of the essentials for survival are shelter, food, water, clothing, and heating. However, no government has established an official poverty line. Traditionally, there are two main concepts of poverty: absolute poverty and relative poverty.

Professor Marsland regarded relative poverty as "pure nonsense" and that such reference was intended to perpetuate Marxist and Socialist criticism of capitalism, rather the comparison be made between countries or cities. Novak's equation of advanced capitalist countries with the Third World may be true only in respect of their inequalities of employment as a determinant of the standard of living. The *difference* is that people in advanced capitalist countries suffer from over-eating related diseases while those in the Third World die from malnutrition.

Inequality is not the same as poverty though both may exist at the same time in occupation within employment. Inequality may be compared with social exclusion although it existed from the feudal days but in modern times it is identified with poverty. Over twenty percent of children in Britain lived in poverty and in 1993 families, three quarters of the total population, lived in poverty below the Income Support level. According to Barnados there are currently – in the first quarter of the twenty-first century – 3.5 million children who live in poverty. Sixty-three percent of children living in poverty are in a family where someone works. The decisive move towards economic construction, notably the social insurance, was based on the Beveridge report and recommendations, with which the modern concept of the welfare state is associated. Its purpose and basic principles on which post-war reform was to be based was reflected in the clear, simple language understood by the many.

Poverty is looked at from different angles: How those who are not poor feel about the poor; who should look after the poor if they cannot look after themselves; the question of a definition of poverty; the growth of population; is poverty confined to certain countries or is it a universal shortcoming; how is genuine poverty balanced with complacency; and whether poverty is as a result of legal and social neglect or social welfare.

The general view is that illness, old age, and inability to work or to find work are the causes of poverty. In Europe the social label in defining poverty has evolved by government policy. In Africa poverty is regarded with indifference, as a way of life. Since the beginning of oral and written history, universally poverty itself has remained immutable despite governmental and charitable efforts to respond to the needy.

The answer depends on the question as to why and how peoples diverged to wealth imbalances universally. The further question is whether Europe has a moral duty to eliminate poverty in the so-called Third World. The main duty first lies with each country to eliminate its own poverty by social engineering and a balanced wealth. Health, education, housing, infrastructure and public amenities in general, lie heavily at the hands of the state, the central political authority and the organised community.

In Europe, there are a number of issues that touch on poverty: the poor have been exploited in false hopes of winning the lottery, on the commercial aspect. The lives of citizens depend on the social policy of government. Twenty-one years on, Bob Geldof found it necessary to repeat the world's greatest concert (02/07/05), to highlight world poverty. The value of the concert was the immediate response to the elimination of poverty but not as a long-term solution, unless aid was practically and gradually transformed into trade exchange in a big way; and the addition of European/African migration exchange in occupational organisation.

The monopoly of poverty does not belong to the Third World. Hurricane Katrina, in Eastern North America, had yet shown the world's vulnerable peoples and the sad face of poverty in the world's most powerful and richest country.

European rule has not been the cause of nineteenth-century under-development and poverty in Africa, rather the subordination of African economy by the mercantile linking of trade to Indian merchant capitalism. But if you take away a people's culture replace it with something of value. The inevitable phenomenon is a changing world and no one can any longer rely on nature alone.

The indifference of the leaders, both European from the nineteenth century, and African in post nineteen-fifties, and the lack of communication and trade exchange between Africa and Europe after the independence of African countries, are among the main causes of the lack of development and chronic poverty in Africa; as some will say to engage in welfare is to reward laziness. This begs the question as to who is poor in any given country?

On the Nordic model the Communist and Nazi movements threatened democracy in most of Europe that followed the depression of the early nineteen thirties. State-guaranteed welfare became the guiding principle in the industrialised Nordic Region of the twentieth century. It does not matter what label we may put on `welfare': job seekers, pension credit or the civil list, or other, they all carry the same value a `benefit' to the recipient, though there is a big *difference* in the lives of prince and pauper. The United Kingdom model is unique in its humanitarian aspect – every geriatric is entitled to receive from the state the non-means tested `Bus Pass', that is to say, literally all, the rich and the poor – here there is no *difference*.

In Britain child poverty is found among poor families or orphans being raised with limited or in some cases absent state resources. In other countries child poverty is a way of life. Under the Child Poverty Act of 2010 the government was to reduce child poverty but this has, not as yet, been achieved. It is estimated that the number of children living in poverty will rise from 2.4 million to 3.4 million by 2020 the set date for elimination of poverty, according to the Institute for Fiscal Studies. It would seem that the reason for poverty in a welfare state, is that the administrators do not take into account the growth of population and make appropriate allowances.

Child poverty rose steeply under Thatcher, and by the time Labour came to power, 3.4 million children were poor. Labour had got that down to 2 million during its 13 years in power; now all the hard-won progress is unravelling. The most infamous cut out of all was the Department of Education's decision to end universal free school milk - taken by Secretary of State Margaret Thatcher before she became Prime Minister. This earned her the title: "Thatcher...Milk Snatcher".

Like everything else there are two sides to every story. In 1958 Harold Wilson's Labour Government took free milk away from secondary schools and from all children over eleven years of age. Though one may say to continue the milk programme for children under eleven was not unreasonable. The lack of milk intake for the child is one that cannot be replaced in adulthood. There are many adults who suffer from Vitamin D deficiency for lack of milk intake during childhood.

Milk is one of the best sources for the human body in childhood: its most valuable content is calcium, strengthens the bones; decreases bone fracture; reduces the risk of decayed teeth and weak gums; contains water molecules which helps to rehydrate the body; contains vitamins, minerals, and carbohydrates which increase energy, protein or body repair and growth; and Vitamin D helps the body absorb calcium.

People in other societies find it hard to believe that child poverty exists in Britain but in reality child poverty in Britain is like an abscess that will not go away, though other countries are worse off. When Mary of Bethany anointed the feet of Jesus one of the men criticised her action and Jesus said:

> "Let her alone...you always have the poor with you, but you do
>
> not always have me."

The latest UNICEF statistics show that the UK situation is much worse than other wealthy developed nations, and that UK ranks sixteenth with Hungary on child poverty. Countries like Ireland, France, Slovenia, Iceland and the Czech Republic achieve lower levels of child poverty.

Poverty has a profound psychological effect on children including their families and society as a whole. Poverty psychologically affects the child's future prospects, be it attainment of education or economic participation. However, the welfare principle is the "golden thread" that runs through decision-making by the United Kingdom courts in the cases of children. The child's upbringing, administration of the child's income and the child's welfare is the paramount consideration of the courts.

If children are caught up in poverty the politicians need to examine their methods. Poverty is not a sickness but a symptom of bad government. The causes of poverty in the first place are moral and in the second economic.

Poverty reflects bad government, but then two things reflect human existence. In the modern sense Google echoes Shakespeare's As You Like it: We log into Google, play our role within, and log out...but we remain ignorant as to how others are affected by the role we play. The world was here when we made our entrance into it, and it is always here when we leave it.

EPILOGUE

Since the early 1960s it became fashionable to deride Britain and other Western powers for colonisation. In our existence, there is nothing wholly good or wholly bad, but a matter of balancing, whether there is more good than bad (Abraham Lincoln). Many ancient atrocities in the colonised areas were removed by colonisation, although an opportunity was lost to create a multi-racial society. But then in that particular era, the *difference* between ruler and ruled, was so great that such a notion was unthinkable. Instead colonialism outlived itself by the inevitable evolution of all things as everything has its time. The presence of Britain, more so than that of her contemporary empires, brought relief and peace in certain aspects including things affecting women. In India a Hindu widow was no longer placed alive on her dead husband's funeral pyre. In other areas of Africa, maidens were no longer chosen to be buried alive with a dead chief to serve and 'comfort' the chief in the land of the dead according to local custom. Slavery, which still existed in the east coast of Africa despite abolition by Britain and America in 1807, came to an end, though in the twenty-first century there is slavery of a different kind, human trafficking. There are seven billion people on this planet in a setting of *differences,* yet the human race is one and *differences* and discrimination made on a *difference* is man-made. In the twenty-first century we live in a culture of unprecedented selfishness at the top as seen in redundancies in most organisations - a worship of Mammon.

In South Africa, despite the death of apartheid, people stick to their own racial groups and there is no inter-mingling of the races, by choice. In Malawi, once they got over "the boot is on the other foot" period after independence, had something to tell the world: there were no race or colour barriers and people mixed and socialised freely as a way of life but this is now changing.

Most of us fail to ask why in creation there are so many *differences* and choose to pass judgments about those who are *different* from us. Has man treated fellow being with compassion? To acknowledge and accept the *difference* is not a denial for people to pursue culture or religion of their choice and *difference* can be celebrated instead.

Above all, the recognition of individual rights is essential. The main consideration is not that an individual should deserve basic rights and protection, to the extent where language is altered for political correctness, but should be accorded equal rights and opportunities within the mainstream society regardless of being there by choice or by accident. A single individual may seem negligible to some but it takes a group of single individuals to make up a community or society as a whole. Most of the privileged in Britain are comprised of past generations of immigrants from different countries in varying circumstances – including the monarchy.

What makes people flock to Britain? After such a long wrangle of seemingly endless debates over the issue of the deportation of Abu Katada (the role model for Britain's humanitarian stance, in July 2013) from Britain much concerned the English judges that Katada would not be free from torture in his country and that he would not receive a fair trial. Such is the humanitarian aspect of the British system of justice.

Or perhaps it is England's welcoming shores, hence on to Scotland, Wales, Ireland and other British Isles. Britain has something to say to the world about values of freedom, democracy (despite the FPTP system!) and the dignity of people, in spite of its immutable sophistry and snobbery. Freedom of speech, provided there is no defamation or impingement on the freedom of others, one's head would remain on one's shoulders – unless treason was committed.

Above all, any person's choice to reject government by fear and coercion and seek to be governed by freedom and affection, is the greatest value Britain offers to immigrants. The British core of fairness is trumpeted beyond the seas even though some are reluctant to admit it.

This expose would be incomplete if I did not include my experience with the Baha'i Community on the teachings of Bahá'u'lláh on unity, equality, and oneness of humanity, which I believe would disarm any kind *difference* and promote peace and harmony in the world. According to the official website of the international Baha'i Community www.bahi.org:

"Since the inception of the Bahá'í Faith in the Nineteenth Century, a growing number of people have found in the teachings of Bahá'u'lláh a compelling vision of a better world. Many have drawn insights from these teachings—for example, on the oneness of humanity, on the equality of women and men, on the elimination of prejudice, on the harmony of science and religion—and have sought to apply Bahá'í principles to their lives and work. Others have gone further and have decided to join the Bahá'í community and participate in its efforts to contribute directly to the realization of Bahá'u'lláh's stupendous vision for humanity's coming of age.

Bahá'ís hail from all walks of life. Young and old, men and women alike, they live alongside others in every land and belong to every nation. They share a common goal of serving humanity and refining their inner-lives in accordance with the teachings of Bahá'u'lláh. The community to which they belong is one of learning and action, free from any sense of superiority or claim to exclusive understanding of truth. It is a community that strives to cultivate hope for the future of humanity, to foster purposeful effort, and to celebrate the endeavours of all those in the world who work to promote unity and alleviate human suffering.

And to quote from 'Abdu'l Baha:

"Bahá'u'lláh has drawn the circle of unity, He has made a design for the uniting of all the peoples, and for the gathering of them all under the shelter of the tent of universal unity. This is the work of the Divine Bounty, and we must all strive with heart and soul until we have the reality of unity in our midst, and as we work, so will strength be given unto us. The earth is one and mankind its citizens."

A social observation of cultures, and the impact of *difference* of any kind has on peoples regardless of rank, as humans sharing a common planet. How Western European ideals influenced other cultures; and the consequence of increased categories of *difference* in the patterns of human behaviour in a changing historical context; the constant running thread of separation of peoples by *difference* in varying degrees; and the widening gap between rich and poor, in both Western European and other societies of the world.